SOCRATIC METHODS

IN THE CLASSROOM

SOCRATIC METHODS

IN THE CLASSROOM

Encouraging Critical Thinking and Problem Solving Through Dialogue

Erick Wilberding, Ph.D.

Routledge
Taylor & Francis Group

NEW YORK AND LONDON

Library of Congress catalog information
currently on file with the publisher.

First published in 2019 by Prufrock Press Inc.

Published in 2021 by Routledge
605 Third Avenue, New York, NY 10017
2 Park Square, Milton Park, Abingdon, Oxon OX14 4RN

Routledge is an imprint of the Taylor & Francis Group, an informa business

Copyright © 2019 Taylor & Francis Group

Cover design by Micah Benson and layout design by Allegra Denbo

ISBN: 9781032142036 (hbk)
ISBN: 9781618218698 (pbk)

DOI: 10.4324/9781003238089

DEDICATION

To the memory of my brother Craig T. Wilberding (1963–2019)

TABLE OF CONTENTS

INTRODUCTION

The Socratic Method is an adaptive strategy of questioning that stimulates personal understanding. I believe that it is one of the most recognized and least understood methods of teaching. It has been adapted to different domains in different ways, and other non-Socratic practices—some helpful for education, and some not so helpful—have become associated with it. Therefore, when someone says, "Socratic Method," he or she is most probably referring to an adaptation, and the adaptations can appear very unalike. Given these variations, it is challenging to discern what is meant by "Socratic Method."

In my first book, *Teach Like Socrates* (Wilberding, 2014), I sought to clarify the essential elements of the Socratic Method by returning to the dialogues of Plato and Xenophon. In reading these fascinating and enriching philosophical texts, one catches glimpses of Socrates, but always through the imagination and intentions of the writers. Socrates left no writings, and he did not engage Plato or Xenophon as a chronicler of his conversations. Their dialogues are literary works, not transcripts; they are performances, not demonstrations. The writers have adapted the Socratic Method to their literary purposes. In a sense, reading about Socrates is like learning about Rembrandt's art by studying only the works by his pupils.

In the ancient world, then, we encounter adaptations of Socratic Methods. There are common elements, but each adaptation uses different selections, applications, and emphases. Today the challenge is to recognize and extract the elements from the literary context, and plant them again within a creative and spontaneous pedagogical and oral context. *Teach Like Socrates* (Wilberding, 2014) explained

DOI: 10.4324/9781003238089-1

how this can be done. *Socratic Methods in the Classroom* complements and extends this explanation by examining some of the most conspicuous adaptations that have taken root and prospered.

The adaptations can be understood as lenses, focused on reasoning, with varied degrees of magnification. An adaptation with a high degree of magnification rigorously and precisely tracks or guides the path of reasoning. An adaptation with a lesser degree of magnification permits more wandering and free interaction in the field of reasoning, but keeps the path focused so that the direction is not lost. There are educational benefits to the use of different lenses on different occasions. For instance, it easier to organize lessons with lesser magnification, permitting more free discussion; within these lessons, however, the teacher can then bring selected ideas into greater focus and development with more rigorous questioning. The teacher begins with lesser magnification, and then applies higher degrees as necessary and helpful. Of course, for this process to be successful, students must also understand how to use the different lenses.

This book clarifies how the Socratic Method has been adapted in the last 400 years in different domains of knowledge and learning. It is not written for philosophers or historians of philosophy who scrutinize the dialogues of Plato and Xenophon. It is written for teachers and seeks to answer the question: How does one teach Socratically?

One-hundred-and-fifty years ago, an answer was better known. There was a shared basic understanding of what constituted the Socratic Method because students read the classics in schools. Educated people read Plato and Xenophon. For many reasons, the classics are not as well represented in the classroom anymore, which means that many teachers and students need an introduction to the Socratic Method and the ancient sources in which it may be found. *Teach Like Socrates* (Wilberding, 2014) was intended as that introduction, and *Socratic Methods in the Classroom* continues the story. Essentially, this story is about problems and questions. Each adaptation approaches a different kind of problem with a different Socratic strategy of questioning.

CHAPTER 1

CRITICAL THINKING

RIGOROUS REASONING WITH BALANCED JUDGMENT

Nevertheless, philosophy has its raison d'être, and one ought to recognize that anyone who has not had some acquaintance with it is hopelessly uneducated.

—Jean Piaget

THE KNOWLEDGE-BASED GLOBAL COMMUNITY

In 2012, Harvard mathematician Samuel Arbesman published *The Half-Life of Facts*, explaining the surprising patterns in the growth of knowledge. The accumulation of knowledge is not a day-by-day, year-by-year, patient sweeping of facts into an ever higher pyramid. In reality, it involves a more fitful, but ultimately predictable, growth that often renders previous knowledge obsolete. Knowledge may decay. What we regard as a fact today may be reclassified as false tomorrow. For example, for decades in the early 20th century, scientists believed there were 48 chromosomes until two independent-minded scientists had the temerity to challenge this conception with a more accurate count of 46. Ingesting radium and

DOI: 10.4324/9781003238089-2

smoking tobacco were once believed to be healthy. Arbesman (2012a) explained how knowledge predictably expands and contracts in trends that can be measured through scientometrics. Knowledge in mathematics, for instance, remains stable for long periods of time, but knowledge in medicine changes often. Generally, knowledge in the social sciences alters more quickly than in the physical sciences. There is no stasis. In a paradigm shift, knowledge might even utterly disappear, replaced by a more complete and useful model (Kuhn, 1962).

This perpetual expansion of knowledge challenges societies to focus the value and purpose of knowledge. On one hand, there is the reality (pithily phrased by Francis Bacon) that knowledge is power. But what kind of power? From one perspective, society's knowledge has become the basis of economic growth and well-being—of economic power. According to Drucker (1999), a knowledge economy is one in which knowledge itself, rather than resources, labor, or capital, becomes the key asset. The news is rife with stories about nations hurrying to innovate their economies to become knowledge-based and therefore more competitive. The World Bank has devised indices, The Knowledge Index (KI) and the Knowledge Economic Index (KEI), that attempt to measure and rank nations according to indicators that include the education and skill of the population.

On the other hand, the value and purpose of knowledge are not restricted to its pragmatic economic impact (Nussbaum, 2010). The expansion of knowledge includes a deepened and more refined awareness of ethical responsibilities—the duties incumbent upon human beings as global citizens. Arbesman's (2012b) study of quantifiable knowledge might also apply to the measurement of ethical knowledge. How does this knowledge grow and decay? Does one measure the extent to which human rights are respected? What about the extent of justice within the world, the degree of freedom within a society, the extent of equality, or the collective happiness in society? How does economic power influence these fundamental aspects of our lives? In order to meet such questions, as well as a host of related ones, we must engage in collective critical thinking. What are human rights? What do we mean by *happiness, equality, freedom,* or *justice*? "Knowledge is power" can inform the fundamental concepts and issues that give meaning to our lives.

In a global community whose knowledge unceasingly grows and decays, the habit and the challenge of critical thinking is urgent. Critical thinking skills impact the growth of nations in all of the ways that grant meaning to life. But what exactly do we mean by *critical thinking*?

RIGOROUS REASONING WITH BALANCED JUDGMENT

The word *critical* often has a negative connotation. Those who are critical seem to be fault-finding and ungenerous in judgment. However, the etymology of the word can be traced from the Latin *criticus* (able to discern or judge) directly to the Greek word κριτικός (able to discern), which in turn is related to κριτής (a judge) as well as to κριτήριον (criterion, a standard for judging). To think critically, then, means to think with balanced or discerning judgment. It is not so much to judge negatively, but to judge well.

However, this short definition can be developed much further. Thinking itself is a complex phenomenon that continues to be investigated (Holyoak & Morrison, 2005, 2012). There are many competing contemporary definitions for critical thinking (Bensley, 2011). In the philosophical tradition, critical thinking is virtually synonymous with training in informal logic. There is close attention to the qualities that constitute what it is to be critical. In the psychological tradition, the focus is on the nature and dynamics of thinking itself. For the eminent psychologist Robert J. Sternberg (1986), "critical thinking comprises the mental processes, strategies, and representations people use to solve problems, make decisions, and learn new concepts" (p. 2). We will look at how these two traditions—the philosophical and psychological—complement and inform each other.

THE PHILOSOPHICAL TRADITION

The philosophical tradition, which emerged from the ancient Greek figures of Plato and Aristotle, views logical reasoning in an ideal situation (Sternberg, 1986). One identifies arguments, their elements, and their structures, probing them for validity and soundness. Since the Middle Ages, logic courses have trained students in this capacity. The 17th century saw the rise of informal logic (i.e., the attempt to apply the basic tools of reasoning, without training in meticulous scholastic logic, to understanding arguments in ordinary daily life), which permitted educated people to reason well (Groarke, 2017). In the 18th century, Isaac Watts (1743), among others, continued this tradition with *The Improvement of the Mind*. In the 19th century, there were similar efforts in presenting reasoning and rhetoric. In 1946, Max Black, a professor of philosophy at Cornell University, published *Critical Thinking: An Introduction to Logic and Scientific Method*, which succinctly presented accessible lessons in deductive logic (including truth tables), language and fallacies, and inductive logic and the scientific method. In addition to examples from contemporary newspapers, magazines, and books, the volume contained summaries, comprehension tests, and exercises for each chapter. It also contained entertaining logic puzzles. Since the 1970s, university courses in critical thinking have proliferated, seeking to draw closer connections between informal logic and reasoning in daily life (Groarke, 2017). These courses focus on how one makes claims and supports them, how one may use or misuse statistics, how reasoning can be cogent or more strictly valid, and how one distinguishes value statements from factual statements. These courses may also cover the biases within the media, including the realities of the Internet, social media, and the strategic use of fake news.

Today a plethora of texts, both popular and scholastic, provide instruction in critical thinking from this point of view (e.g., Browne & Keeley, 2015; Kelley, 2014; Schick & Vaughn, 2014; Swatridge, 2014). In different orders and to different extents, these texts address the elements of argument and justification, deductive and inductive reasoning (and perhaps abductive reasoning as well), logical fallacies, and issues concerning values. Some texts go into great technical detail (e.g., Kelley 2014). Some texts restrict themselves to explanations of the essential critical thinking skills and concepts, whereas others (e.g., Moore & Parker, 2016) present a comprehensive textbook replete with exercises that will keep any class meaningfully busy for a semester or more. The exercises in these books are drawn from current affairs, bridging the chasm between theory and practice and making clear the relevance of the skills.

Moreover, several tests have been composed to assess an individual's general ability for critical thinking (Ennis, 1993). One of the better known assessments, the Watson-Glaser Critical Thinking Appraisal, was first assembled in the 1940s by Goodwin Barbour Watson and Edward Maynard Glaser, and has been modified and maintained over several decades (Ennis, 1958, 1993; Glaser, 1941; Gordon, 1993, 1994). An appraisal that is more appropriate for high school students, and one used by selected faculties at Oxford University for screening applicants, is the Thinking Skills Assessment (the Oxford TSA), which measures problem-solving skills, including numerical and spatial reasoning, as well as the ability to understand and judge arguments (Cambridge Assessment Admissions Testing, 2019). Both of these appraisals attempt to quantify an individual's ability to recognize assumptions, evaluate arguments, make inferences, deduce, and interpret reasonably. Ennis (1993) gave suggestions as to how a teacher might compose his or her own test of critical thinking.

Matthew Lipman (1988a) presented this philosophical tradition of critical thinking to children and documented the positive impact it made on education. Through the discussion of carefully composed philosophical novels (seven in all), Lipman sought to awaken and develop children's reasoning skills in order to create a community of inquiry. For Lipman (1988b), critical thinking was "skillful, responsible thinking that facilitates good judgment because it (1) relies upon criteria, (2) is self-correcting, and (3) is sensitive to context" (p. 39).

SUMMARY
Critical Thinking in the Philosophical Tradition

- ▸ Critical thinking generally means training in informal logic.

- ▸ Students learn the elements of deductive and inductive argument and valid reasoning, including the awareness of assumptions, consequences, and implications.

- ▸ Students learn about logical fallacies.

- ▸ Students learn about precision in the use and interpretation of language.

- ▸ Thinking appraisal tests attempt to quantify the level of students' ability to understand and assess arguments.

THE PSYCHOLOGICAL TRADITION

The psychological tradition describes how critical thinking "is performed under the limitations of the person and the environment," that is, how people think with limited information, time, etc. (Sternberg, 1986, p. 5). In the last 30 years, continuing advances within cognitive psychology, developmental psychology, and neuroscience have contributed fascinating insights about how human beings think (Holyoak & Morrison, 2005, 2012). There has been increased public understanding of dual processing, cognitive biases, and the maturation of reasoning and judgment.

DUAL PROCESSING AND COGNITIVE BIASES

In 2002, Daniel Kahneman won the Nobel Prize "for having integrated insights from psychological research into economic science, especially concerning human judgment and decision-making under uncertainty" (The Nobel Foundation). In 2011, he published *Thinking Fast and Slow*, which summarized his research, conducted with his friend Amos Tversky, on dual processing. Tversky and Kahneman distinguished two interacting systems: System 1 and System 2. The first is intuitive, associative, effortless, and automatic. It makes instant decisions, permitting us to navigate through the day without the burden of extensive analysis and evaluation. "System 1 has been shaped by evolution," Kahneman (2011) wrote, "to provide a continuous assessment of the main problems that an organism must solve to survive: How are things going? Is there a threat or a major opportunity? Should I approach or avoid?" (p. 90). System 2, in contrast, is slow, deliberate, and effortful reasoning, moving logically from premise to premise to reach a reasonable conclusion. It is discursive and reflective, making distinctions and seeking evidence for conclusions.

As human beings, using System 1 thinking, we rely on heuristics in reasoning and decision making. A heuristic is a short, time-saving process for arriving quickly at a solution or judgment. However, heuristics also predictably generate cognitive biases that condition and distort judicious reasoning. For instance, given our existing frames of reference and beliefs, we tend to interpret new situations or information in a manner consistent with these beliefs, which may compel us to ignore significant information. This is called *confirmation bias*. We filter new information to confirm our existing beliefs, interpreting the world around us in terms of our mental map. Yet, as the philosopher Alfred Korzybski (1958) memorably said, "the map is not the territory" (p. 58). There is always more to be apprehended beyond the simple or intricate mental maps that shape our interpretations. Another common bias, which is relevant for anyone teaching inductively, is *anchoring bias*, which refers to the tendency to rely and make judgments based on the first information received. *Saliency bias* is the tendency to make judgments or to forge attitudes based on dramatic events that grab our attention. Influenced by the media or our own experience, we make judgments based on striking but statistically improbable events. *Availability bias* refers to the tendency to rely only on the information that is immediately within reach, and not to actively explore. *Bandwagon bias* is the tendency to assent to the belief of the majority. Critical thinking, or reasoning with balanced judgment, is effortful and prone to errors due to these subtle cognitive biases.

MATURATION IN REASONING AND JUDGMENT

Insights on critical thinking are found in the paradigm of intellectual and ethical development suggested by William G. Perry, Jr. For 33 years, Perry led the Bureau of Study Counsel at Harvard University, and in the 1950s and 1960s he conducted a long-range study, the results of which he published in *Forms of Intellectual and*

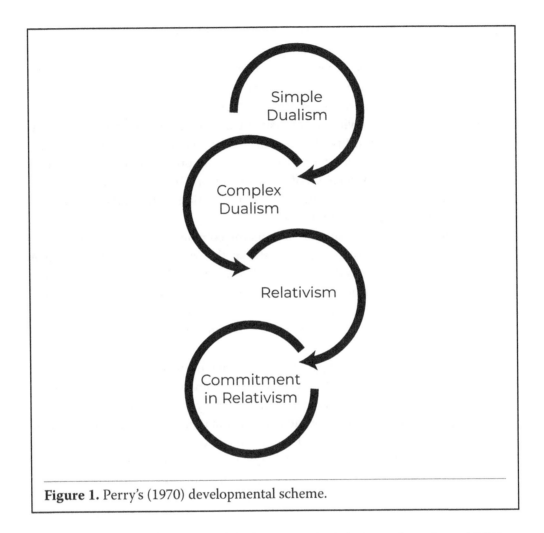

Figure 1. Perry's (1970) developmental scheme.

Ethical Development in the College Years, a book hailed as a modern classic (Gilligan, Kegan, & Sizer, 1999; Perry, 1970).

Perry's (1970) study charts three large phases of critical thinking: dualism (both simple and complex), relativism, and commitment in relativism (see Figure 1). These three broad phases are further articulated into nine positions (we may think of them as mindsets) through which students construct knowledge and values. The first mindset is a simple dualism in which there is always a clear-cut and absolute right or wrong answer; if there is an interpretation, there is a "correct" interpretation of which an authority approves. In its pure state, this mindset is uncommon even in the freshman year of college; students have developed beyond this mindset. The first half of Perry's developmental schema shows the gradual modification of dualism.

The second mindset perceives multiple viewpoints but does not regard them as legitimate or warranted; students still believe in a single correct answer or interpretation (Perry, 1970). There are two expressions of this mindset. First, there is the belief that the multiplicity of interpretations may be caused by an ineffective authority (i.e., teacher) who has not properly expressed the correct view; encountering this, the student may resist the confusion of pluralism by establishing a wall of opposition. A second expression of this mindset is the view that the presentation of multiplicity is only an invitation to discover independently the correct answer. The introduction to complexity, the student believes, is for the student's good. At times, students believe that math and the sciences are precise and procedural disciplines untainted by the vagueness of the humanities. The chaos of multiplicity is believed to be only temporary. However, the perception of multiplicity, however conditioned, opens a new path to doubt.

In the third mindset, the student accepts the complexity, diversity, and uncertainty of multiplicity, but retains the belief that this state is temporary, and that the authority has not yet found the answer (Perry, 1970). The student believes that there will be a correct answer when the authority reaches it. The student is puzzled, though, at how the teacher can grade work for which there is no correct answer. The student believes that either more generalizations or more facts are needed to receive a better grade.

The fourth mindset, which appeared on average in the spring of the students' first year at college, views diversity of opinion as legitimate but subordinate to dualism (Perry, 1970). The student construes this diversity to mean that everyone has a right to an opinion. Within this mindset, students then branch into two tendencies—the tendency to opposition and the tendency to adherence. The former tendency regards authority as bigoted and dogmatic, and demands reasons and evidence. The latter tendency is more docile and conforms more to authority, readily acquiring skills in analysis and judgment, always with the conviction that "this is the way They want you to think" (p. 101). The students acquire the skills of independent thought, but as yet have not entirely embraced this independence.

Perry (1970) moreover identified ways in which progress in the schema may be avoided; development is not an inevitable process of maturation. Within the first three mindsets, through anger, despair, and alienation, students may take refuge in the reassuring certainty of dualism. They may adhere to or oppose authority. In the fourth mindset, students may display an intellectual detachment in the face of pluralism, and the bright student may be skilled in understanding the demands of the assignments and assessments, completing them adeptly but without conviction or commitment. In other words, the student may produce work with all of the hallmarks of independent thought, but only in emulation.

One of the more fascinating insights of Perry's (1970) study is that students are encouraged to mature in critical thinking by their peers. It is not only the experience of the classroom and curriculum that contributes to the development of critical thinking. Outside of the classroom, interaction with students who have better assimilated the skills of critical thinking also stimulates growth in thinking.

In the fifth mindset, relativism is regarded as intrinsically correct (Perry, 1970). The authority takes its place within this new qualified understanding. The last four mindsets are:

- ▸ more personally coming to terms with the relativism of knowledge and foreseeing a commitment in relativism (sixth mindset),
- ▸ making an initial commitment (seventh mindset),
- ▸ orienting oneself within the implications of these commitments (eighth mindset), and
- ▸ developing these commitments further (ninth mindset).

Perry observed that 75% of the class sample attained the commitments of the seventh and eighth mindsets.

The conclusions of this study are immensely helpful for understanding the responses of students to a range of issues. We can understand students in high school as experiencing the first few phases of this paradigm. Students may be entrenched within dualism, moving into complex dualism, or beginning to understand relativism. Even the very brightest of students, who are particularly gifted in manipulating abstract ideas, will not have the experience as yet to make more sophisticated personal commitments that are outlined in commitment within relativism. The paradigm suggests how intellectual development may inform our teaching strategies. A strategy that emphasizes convergent thinking, or the search for the right answer, affirms the dualistic thinking that relies on an authority. On the other hand, strategies that bring other points of view into light for exploration and evaluation foster movement into the next phase.

REFLECTIVE JUDGMENT

King and Kitchener (1994, 2002) suggested another insightful paradigm for the maturation of thinking, called *reflective judgment*. As adolescents and adults encounter ill-structured problems, they have discernable reactions or positions that may be understood in a structure of three levels: prereflective thinking, quasi-reflective thinking, and reflective thinking.

In *prereflective thinking*, there are three stages (King & Kitchener, 1994). In the first, knowledge is not understood as abstract, but rather is physical, absolute, and apprehended through observation; therefore, it needs no justification, and alternative points of view are not perceived. In the second stage, knowledge is absolute but may not be accessible; it is obtained through sensory perception or through an authority. There is still no need to justify knowledge other than through the senses or through an authority. In the third stage, knowledge is certain, and if one perceives uncertainty, this condition is understood to be transient and one must rely upon personal knowledge until certainty is reestablished through an authority. If there is not an authority with a defined view, then there is only personal opinion, and all opinions are equally valid.

In the next phase, *quasi-reflective thinking*, there are two stages (King & Kitchener, 1994). In the first stage, knowledge is uncertain, and each individual has a personal point of view; beliefs are justified through reasons and evidence acceptable to each person. In the next stage, knowledge is subjective, determined by the individual's perception and standards for judgment; myriad interpretations are known, but there is no certain knowledge. Beliefs are justified within specific contexts and situations.

The final phase, *reflective thinking*, also consists of two stages (King & Kitchener, 1994). In the first stage, there is the awareness that knowledge is constructed from the analysis and evaluation of information derived from a spectrum of sources, as well as from expert interpretations subjected to analysis and evaluation. Justification is based upon the comparison of reasoning and evidence, as well as the application of appropriate criteria. In the next stage, there is the awareness that knowledge is constructed and provisional, subject to revision with the discovery of new evidence, better reasoning, or the creation of innovative means of inquiry. Justification requires weighing a complex series of considerations, dependent upon the type of problem or issue. The best of conclusions are regarded as tentative.

The findings of King and Kitchener (1994) permit a general understanding of how adolescents reason. King and Kitchener found that high school students generally evidenced prereflective thinking. The students regarded knowledge as absolute, certain, and dependent upon authority. At the same time, it is important to remember that high school students generally have not been exposed to how knowledge is constructed and justified. The conscious study of how knowledge is constructed may be touched upon within different classes to different degrees, and it is a declared focus of the International Baccalaureate's obligatory Theory of Knowledge course. However, a sophisticated understanding of the differing ways in which knowledge is constructed and justified presupposes a level of metacognition or informed philosophical reflection that generally is not present within secondary education. King and Kitchener found that students in college exhibited movement from prereflective to quasi-reflective thinking, whereas graduate students generally exhibited quasi-reflective and reflective thinking.

King and Kitchener (2002) offered several insightful suggestions for teaching, including:

   ▸ showing respect for the student's developmental stage regarding how knowledge is created and justified;

- discussing controversial issues founded upon a clear and shared understanding of the facts and different interpretations of the facts;
- creating opportunities for the analysis and evaluation of alternative points of view;
- teaching strategies for the gathering, analysis, and evaluation of data that permit judgments; and
- applying thinking skills in a variety of contexts beyond the classroom (p. 55).

NEUROSCIENCE

Lastly, through technological advances in neuroimaging and other means of inquiry, neuroscience has helped us understand better how the human brain functions, and it promises many insights in the years to come that will affect education policy as well as teaching and learning (Organisation for Economic Co-operation and Development [OECD], 2007). Recently, brain research has attracted major financial support in the hope and expectation that it will benefit understanding of the human body as the Human Genome Project did. In 2013, the United States funded a long-term project called Brain Research through Advancing Innovative Neurotechnologies (BRAIN). In the same year, the European Union funded the Human Brain Project. Most recently, the International Brain Initiative (IBI) was established to better coordinate communication and efforts within the global community of brain researchers. Brain research, for reasons that go beyond its impact on education, is becoming a priority in today's world.

Developments have permitted the discarding of common myths, such as left brain versus right brain, the belief that humans use only 10% of their brains, and the belief that the brain is determined by the age of 3 (United Nations Educational, Scientific and Cultural Organization, 2007). Developing neuroscience also has contributed to our understanding of how memory functions and how dependent it is on understanding.

Research has also increased understanding of the development of the brain during adolescence (Blakemore, 2012; Blakemore & Frith, 2005; Jensen, 2005; OECD, 2007). In particular, we now know that there is growth of white matter in the frontal cortex, the part of the brain associated with executive functions, such as planning and selecting actions. Accompanying this, there is synaptic pruning, which is associated with the fine-tuning of functions. Blakemore and Frith (2005) suggested devoting more educational time to the evaluation of transmitted knowledge during this phase of development. In other words, the natural process of brain development that adolescents undergo would benefit from an increased focus on critical thinking.

SUMMARY
Critical Thinking in the Psychological Tradition

- ▸ There is more awareness of the dynamics and difficulties of thinking.

- ▸ Thinking can be imagined as two systems. The first is intuitive, automatic, emotional, and given to generalizations. The second is deliberate, slow, rational, and effortful.

- ▸ Cognitive biases may influence and inhibit our reasoning and judgment.

- ▸ Perry (1970) charted a common development in intellectual and ethical maturity in the college years, as students pass from dependence on authority to an autonomous and aware commitment within a pluralistic world. High school students may be seen at the beginning of this continuum.

- ▸ King and Kitchener (1994, 2002) suggested a developmental paradigm called *reflective judgment*. Like Perry (1970), they found that high school students generally fall into the level of prereflective thinking (i.e., believing that knowledge is fixed, absolute, and learned from authority).

- ▸ Neuroscience offers new insights on how we think and on the continuing physical development of the adolescent brain. Increased maturation in the prefrontal cortex is associated with executive judgment.

THE CHALLENGE OF FOSTERING CRITICAL THINKING

From this overview, we see that the understanding of critical thinking has two dimensions. There is a normative dimension within the philosophical tradition and a descriptive one within the psychological tradition. Educators must be aware of both dimensions so we can better frame and understand the realities, the possibilities, and the necessities for our students in developing a capacity for critical thinking.

In the philosophical tradition, the principles of logical reasoning, or higher level thinking, are articulated in terms of analysis, synthesis, and evaluation. Teachers and students may understand what makes a convincing or persuasive argument. Teaching critical thinking, however, must go beyond the cultivation of the skills of informal logic or general thinking skills. Different domains of knowledge, which construct knowledge through different methodologies, may call upon different ways of thinking and may have different convictions for what constitutes evidence. For instance, experimental or observational science is conducted within an empirical-inductive paradigm and depends in part on the principle of falsifiability. History, on the other hand, requires teachers and students to gather and consider evidence in a different manner.

The psychological tradition provides many insights that illuminate daily experience in the classroom. Theories of epistemological development sketch a framework in which to understand the positions and possibilities of the students. In general, adolescents exhibit a dualistic or prereflective level of thinking. The challenge for teachers is to scaffold thoughtful consideration of alternative ways of interpretation, analysis, and evaluation.

Language instruction also plays a powerful role in developing critical thinking within a pluralistic society. Gallagher (2008) underlined the necessity and efficacy of embracing the primary culture and language of students. In the United States, more than 4 million students study English as a second language, and this number is growing (National Center for Education Statistics, 2018). By the 2030s, this group is projected to account for 40% of the school-age population (Thomas & Collier, 2002). A student's first culture and language should be affirmed and partnered with the second language. Thomas and Collier (1997) demonstrated that students have greater academic success when the curriculum addresses language development in this manner. The entire school environment should be structured to permit this natural growth.

The Socratic Method offers the means to guide the development of rigorous reasoning in this pluralistic society in which knowledge of all kinds is continuously developing. Knowledge within different domains is constructed and tested in different ways. Ill-structured problems or controversial issues require rigorous reasoning and therefore nudge students forward in maturity. The adaptations of the Socratic Method to different domains require its alignment with the manner of critical thinking proper to each domain.

The Socratic Method is not merely a means of applying normative tests to our thinking in different domains. The Socratic Method also offers modern insights into learning. It may be adapted to modern learning activities and experiences that foster greater engagement. In the next chapter, we will see how this growth in understanding operates in the classroom. It is often more helpful to speak of multiple Socratic Methods rather than one Socratic Method.

CHAPTER 2

FROM SOCRATIC METHOD TO SOCRATIC METHODS

> The matters that are suitable for treatment by the Socratic Method are those as to which we have already enough knowledge to come to a right conclusion, but have failed, through confusion of thought or lack of analysis, to make the best logical use of what we know.
>
> —Bertrand Russell

INTERPRETATIONS AND ADAPTATIONS

If we look at portrait busts of Socrates, we see a variety of likenesses. Ancient sculptors interpreted his features in different ways. Socrates was very far from the classical ideal of harmonious beauty seen in the famous bronze or marble sculptures of the fifth century BCE. With his bulging eyes and snub nose, he was affectionately teased for resembling a satyr or Silenus, the chubby god of wine. The spectrum of portraits presents these qualities in different ways and with different emphases. Some are very broadly carved; others are more meticulous, dignified, and quite elegant. But which best represents the features of the historical Socrates?

DOI: 10.4324/9781003238089-3

The variety of depictions is analogous to the variety of understandings and adaptations of Socrates's philosophical method of questioning. There are resemblances and divergences among interpretations by educators from different time periods and locations. Cultural context, the domain of knowledge, and the specific purpose of questioning contribute to expressions of the Socratic Method. Some elements are emphasized, and others are deemphasized or are missing altogether. The expectation of whether a teacher instructs an individual, a small group, or a larger class also has shaped the method's interpretation and application. Lastly, an individual teacher's mastery and style affect how Socratic questioning is used and adapted.

The two questions we must answer to understand interpretations and adaptations of the Socratic Method are: *Socratic in what way? Socratic to what extent?* In this chapter, we will review how Socrates questioned his followers. We will then overview some of the ways in which his questioning strategy has been modified in history and today. From this discussion, we will see that it is more often appropriate to speak of Socratic Methods rather than the Socratic Method.

WHAT IS THE SOCRATIC METHOD?

Socrates wrote nothing and perhaps distrusted the written word, whose interpretation and intention could not be clarified in spontaneous exchange. For Socrates, each conversation was a unique performance—unscripted, unrecorded, unrepeatable. But a few of his associates did not share his aversion to writing. Among these were Plato and Xenophon. For years they conversed with Socrates, and they understood and assimilated his unique method of questioning in different ways. Both wrote many dialogues in which Socrates is the protagonist. To understand the Socratic Method, we must begin with their dialogues.

Generally, it is agreed that Plato is the superior philosopher and literary artist. He defined paths of philosophy and raised fundamental issues that are still explored today. Complex, subtle, and profoundly insightful, his dialogues are sophisticated literary masterpieces, not transcripts of conversations; he carefully and artfully selected the place and the company for each discussion of a philosophical problem. Granting the literary license taken, he nonetheless presented the essential elements and dynamics of the challenging conversations of Socrates.

EXAMPLE TEXT: *MENO*

Let us look briefly at an instructive example text, *Meno*, a short, accessible, and often playful dialogue about virtue and knowledge, as well as teaching and learning. This dialogue presents two ways of approaching the Socratic Method; one is applied to a philosophical question, and the other to a question of geometry (the second will be explored in Chapter 3). In the text, Meno, a young aristocrat from Thessaly, asks Socrates: Can virtue can be taught, or is it not teachable but learned through practice? Or, is it an innate quality that people have by nature? Socrates replies that he does not know what virtue is and that one must know this before answering these questions, just as one must know who Meno is before knowing whether he is well-born, rich, and good-looking. Filled with curiosity, Socrates asks what Meno thinks virtue is, and the young man offers a variety of examples: the diverse virtues of a man, a woman, a child, an old man, a free man, or a slave. But this series does not satisfy Socrates, who wants a comprehensive analytic definition expressing the concept of virtue.

Socrates, however, does not bluntly confront and contradict the young aristocrat. He does not lecture. Rather, he demonstrates the inadequacy of Meno's explanation through a series of leading questions and analogies. This step-by-step reasoning leads Meno to the discovery that the diverse examples he offered do not express what virtue essentially is in itself.

Falling back on the definition of virtue once heard from the philosopher Gorgias, Meno then suggests that virtue is the capacity to command others. But Socrates tests this definition by asking whether this would hold true for a child or a slave. Frustrated, Meno asks for clarification on what is meant by "definition," and Socrates provides two examples with the concepts of color and shape. Meno then attempts a third definition—that virtue is to desire beautiful things and to be capable of obtaining them. Again, by means of an inductive series of questions, Socrates insightfully dismantles this definition. Meno is left perplexed. In a famous passage, he compares Socrates to an electric ray fish whose sting numbs the person. The discussion continues, passing from the problem of virtue to a problem of geometry (in order to examine an issue of knowledge).

ELEMENTS OF THE SOCRATIC METHOD

There is a wealth of pedagogical wisdom to gain from Plato's dialogue. First, *friendly and witty conversation* is the medium of education; there is a congenial and cooperative give-and-take that avoids the competitive thrust and parry of debate. This dialogue is not a caustic inquisition. There is also no lecture. Meno learns to think more critically about virtue by thinking aloud with Socrates. The conversation, in this case, is between two people, not among a small or a large group. Socratic reasoning is a social activity.

The two *explore a philosophical issue or problem* that is open, abstract, and universal in appeal, and which requires rational inquiry (to appropriate the four characteristics of philosophical questions suggested by Tozzi [1999]). The question of virtue cannot be resolved through the discovery of a fact. It is not a scientific question. Nor is it a religious question. The philosophical issue is personally meaningful and important to Meno. Socrates does not impose it on him.

Having articulated a philosophical problem, Socrates and Meno then *examine and test a sequence of attempted responses*. Each response, in a sense, is a hypothesis and becomes another problem for analysis and evaluation. Thus, the dialogue is structured as a series of philosophical problems that must be probed and explored. Structuring a conversation around problems is another Socratic strategy.

Each analysis begins with Meno's point of view, his intuitive understanding of what defines virtue. When his *intuition is further articulated and tested*, he sees that the issue is more complex than he realized and requires more careful reasoning and deliberation. There is no preliminary lecture setting out basic ideas. In Kahneman's (2011) terms, Meno offers an intuitive System 1 answer (fast thinking), and Socrates assists in an agile, collaborative, and discursive System 2 exploration of the answer (slow thinking).

Socrates refrains from answering the central question. He claims that he does not know the answer. This *Socratic ignorance* is one of the most enduring characteristics of the Socratic Method (whereas others may be discarded or deemphasized in later adaptations). Socrates helps the thinking process along in many ways, usually through questions of different kinds, but he does not make statements. The burden of thinking is on Meno. With the help of Socrates, Meno must analytically understand and make a series of judgments.

Enthusiastic curiosity is another element of the Socratic Method that it is highly important pedagogically. Socrates is deeply and sincerely interested in Meno's views. He wants to learn more. This is not simply playing upon the vanity of others (although there are times in the dialogues when Socrates does so). Often, when encountering sharp skepticism and doubt from others, people naturally lose the desire to share their thoughts and reasoning. After all, what is the point of sharing ideas with a radical skeptic? Socrates, however, appears sincerely interested and excited about Meno's ideas. His curiosity is balanced by a degree of gentle skepticism necessary for critical thinking. Pólya (1963), whose writings on teaching are permeated with a Socratic spirit, commented on how students may occasionally learn more from a teacher's attitudes than from the subject matter taught. Curiosity and enthusiasm, not caustic and unrelenting doubt, animate the Socratic conversation (Simon, 1966).

Socrates guides *analysis* and *evaluation*; he explores higher level thinking to arrive at a judgment. Conceptually he clarifies what a claim means, where it comes from (i.e., what are the latent assumptions?), and where it is going (i.e., what are the consequences and implications?). He does not quiz for subject information. In guiding the analysis and evaluation, Socrates, for the most part, is not using the vocabulary of contemporary informal logic. Nor is he using question prompts. Each tentative response that Meno makes is handled in a different manner. Although the dialogue is a literary performance, Socrates's approach to Meno nonetheless expresses the advice given by Warren (1942), an eminent modern practitioner of the Socratic Method, that the instructor "must be able to catch as catch can. He must be able to adjust himself, and quickly to adjust himself, to anything that a student may say—developing the good, demolishing the bad" (p. 23). Socrates adjusts himself to the responses of the other person.

"How would that work? Can you walk me through that step by step?" are the kinds of questions that Greco (2010e) advised moderators to ask participants in a discussion. In this way, students must think aloud and manifest the reasoning behind a claim. This is what Socrates is achieving through his *sequences of leading questions*: he walks step by step through the reasoning with the other person. A logical sequence of small agreements, statement by statement, proposition by proposition, makes the analysis and evaluation visible. At times, Socrates offers a choice: "Do you mean this, or do you mean . . . ?" He compares and contrasts. In this way, latent contradictions and inconsistencies are discovered. When he encounters an incorrect claim, Socrates does not bluntly tell Meno that he is wrong and then supply the correct answer. Together they work through the ideas and discover whether the hypothesis is right or wrong. For instance, when Meno defines virtue as being able to desire beautiful things and having the power to acquire them, Socrates walks him through a path of reasoning to clarify the thought, discover his intended meaning, and to discern any contradictions. Moving statement by statement, Socrates begins with the issue of desire and its objects: Do men who desire beautiful things desire good things? Do some men desire bad things? Do they understand that these things are bad? The path of reasoning moves through several statements to arrive at the conclusion: No one wants what is bad unless he wants to be miserable. Then, in the same manner, Socrates and Meno examine the second part of the definition—namely that virtue is the power of securing good things. The definition proves unsatisfactory.

In examining ideas, Socrates makes abundant use of *examples*. He was notorious for using everyday examples familiar to his audience. When Meno gives his examples of virtue—one for a man, and another for a woman, and so forth—Socrates rejects this as unsatisfactory and uses the example of health. There is not one health for a man and another for a woman. The form of health is the same for everyone.

Likewise, there is not one strength for a woman and another for a man. In the same way, Meno must define what virtue would be for all.

Socrates also makes abundant use of *counterexamples* in two ways. First, when someone defines a concept, Socrates tests the definition by suggesting a *counterexample that clearly is appropriate but does not fit the definition*. For instance, in a dialogue that attempts to define courage, Laches says that the courageous man is the one who stands and fights, and holds his post. Socrates gives counterexamples of soldiers who fight by strategically retreating, such as Scythian horseman, Aeneas, or the Spartan hoplites at Plataea. Secondly, Socrates suggests a *counterexample that does fit the definition but clearly is not appropriate*. For instance, when Meno suggests that virtue means being able to command over all, Socrates asks how virtue then can be the same for a child or a slave. Is he who rules still a slave? Meno must admit not. Here, there is no long path of reasoning; rather, a straightforward counterexample compels Meno to understand how the definition fails.

Socrates uses *analogies* to clarify his meaning. At the beginning of the dialogue, when Meno offers many examples of virtues instead of defining what virtue is, Socrates uses an analogy of a swarm of bees. Socrates does not want to know the different kinds of bees and what distinguishes each from the other; he wants to know in what way they are the same (i.e., what makes each a bee). At the end of the dialogue, when Socrates wishes to express how knowledge is superior to true belief, he makes a clever and witty analogy to statues created by Daedalus. Statues by Daedalus were so lifelike that they moved; in the same way, true beliefs that are not grounded with reason are not fixed but move around. These beliefs need to be fixed in place by an understanding of why they are true.

Socrates uses *hypothetical situations* ("What if . . . ?") to test a concept, a rule, or a principle. For instance, in the first book of Plato's *The Republic*, Cephalus defines justice as speaking the truth and paying one's debts. Socrates tests this definition with the hypothetical situation of a sane man who gives his weapons to a friend but then loses his sanity and demands his weapon back. A just friend should not return the weapon to the insane man, for the insane man would harm himself or others. In the same way, no one should feel compelled to tell the whole truth to someone out of his mind.

There is an *open ending*. In the end, frustratingly, Meno learns that he does not really understand virtue. But he has gained new insights into what it is not, and he may have a better understanding of how to test his answers. The exploration never reaches a final destination. What the attentive person obtained was not a new nugget of information, but an understanding of how to analyze and evaluate. Meno now knows what a proper answer would resemble. He understands better how to make the path.

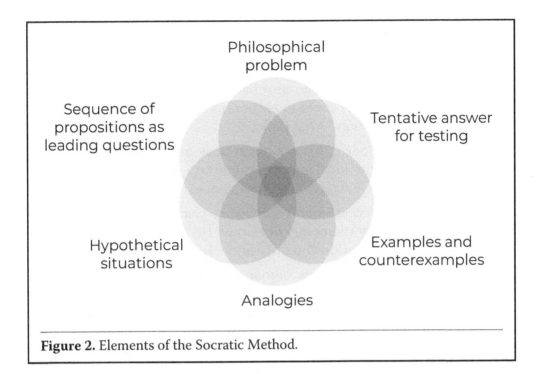

Figure 2. Elements of the Socratic Method.

A Venn diagram can serve as a useful graphic in understanding the mixing of elements within a Socratic conversation (see Figure 2). There is no set progression as Socrates reacts to the other person's statements. Different definitions by different people in different contexts require different elements and combinations. Socratic ignorance and Socratic curiosity are constant elements, and there are always sequences of questions for shared inquiry. Problems always structure the conversation, but there is a creative selection in the moment.

Here it is interesting to remember that Socrates modelled and demonstrated the art of questioning, and, in this way, imparted it primarily to young men, not to teachers. These men assimilated a routine or process of logical reasoning with good judgment about ethical issues.

DIALOGUES FOR STUDY

It is crucial to have read at least one dialogue by Plato. The following four suggestions for reading are not very long, varying from 11 to 30 pages. By reading them, you will better understand the necessary characteristics of the Socratic Method. Naturally, one should read all of the dialogues if possible, although there is more pedagogical wisdom in some dialogues than others.

- ▸ *Euthyphro.* Socrates is waiting before the court that must make the first investigations into the charges against him. He encounters Euthyphro, who has come to accuse his father of homicide. The two explore the question "What is piety?"

- ▸ *The Republic: Book I.* This is the first book of *The Republic*, in which Plato outlines the ideal state. In the house of Polemarchus, with a group of friends, Socrates explores the question "What is justice?"

- ▸ *Ion.* Ion is a successful and somewhat vain professional reciter of poetry, especially the poetry of Homer. He and Socrates investigate the issue of knowledge and inspiration. This is a very short dialogue.

- ▸ *Alcibiades.* Alcibiades was perhaps the most scandalous figure of his time. Handsome, wealthy, and well-born, he was a follower of Socrates in his youth, but later his actions as a general during the Peloponnesian War brought him into disrepute. He passed to the Spartan side and later was in the employ of the Persians. In this dialogue, he and Socrates investigate how virtue is necessary for statesmanship. Some scholars believe the dialogue was written by another philosopher (not Plato), but it held a special place in the ancient world.

ADAPTATIONS AND VARIATIONS OF THE SOCRATIC METHOD

In the ancient world, the Socratic Method first developed through the examination of ethical issues. Socrates eschewed the speculations of those attempting to understand the physical world. Even today, some claim that the Socratic Method only manifests itself in explorations of ethics (Reich, 2003). However, Plato himself adapted Socratic questioning to a problem of geometry, a field of knowledge that likely did not interest the historical Socrates. In the Renaissance, following the rediscovery of the writing of Xenophon and Plato, Socratic pedagogy reemerged. Its extent and precise nature are difficult to ascertain, but in a classically educated world, there were teachers in each century who understood its demands and possibilities. Throughout history, there are mentions of its use, general descriptions, precepts for its use, and testimonies to great teachers who educated Socratically.

There is increasingly more detailed evidence in the present day. It is clear that the Socratic Method surfaces in philosophy, but it embraces and finds expression in many other domains.

DIFFERENT PROBLEMS, DIFFERENT ELEMENTS

Since the Renaissance, many have freely adapted the Socratic Method to diverse domains. Each adaptation borrowed or emphasized different elements of the Socratic Method, according to the objectives of the domain in terms of knowledge, interpretation, reasoning, evidence, and judgment. What changed from domain to domain were the nature of the problem and the manner of thinking. Ill-structured problems remained central, but these problems were not philosophical. Although the testing of intuitions remained in most adaptations, there was often a body of knowledge for which a student was accountable, and well-reasoned positions were subject to Socratic probing. Therefore, fact-based or observation-based questions entered the sequences, as well as specific terminology and methodology. The teacher guided and tested analysis and evaluation within a defined and expanding body of knowledge. Details mattered. There were right and wrong answers. As knowledge developed in domains, so did the application of the Socratic Method.

TEACHING AND POLEMICS OF RELIGION

In the early modern period, the Socratic Method was often presented in logic texts as a means to reveal and refute the errors of other religious creeds (Brightland, 1759; Dalham, 1762; Le Clerc, 1700). In this context, it was not so much a means for teaching, but an adversarial means of debate. The problems under consideration were the religious doctrines of other denominations. Jean Le Clerc (1700), a Remonstrant scholar from Geneva who settled in Amsterdam, recommended following three precepts. Brightland (1759) later translated the precepts into English, which, in more modern English, may be rendered in this manner:

1. Behave in such a way as if one desired to learn something from the person with whom one argues.
2. If the person with whom one speaks makes use of obscure words, one must ask him for their explanation.
3. One must ask questions on the particulars of all of the parts of the doctrine, and their consequences, not as if we find fault in something in them, but that we might more fully understand his teaching; so that he should appear

the teacher, and we the learners. At this point, use examples and analogies, and ask whether he means this or that (pp. 287–288).

In a far less polemical vein, the celebrated poet George Herbert (1652) adapted the Socratic Method to reviewing the teaching of Christian doctrine. His aim was to awaken personal understanding of doctrine, not parroting of formulas. Writing for an educated clerical audience, he advised selecting "an aim and mark of the whole discourse, whither to drive the Answerer, which the Questionist must have in his mind before any question be propounded, upon which and to which the questions are to be chained" (p. 86). Herbert advised using plain language and familiar illustrations. His rapid series of questions, in a short illustration, gives new perspective on the pious poet. One-hundred-and-fifty years later, Immanuel Kant (1803/2007) also recommended the Socratic Method for the formation of reasoning and the teaching of religion. Herbert and Kant, although writing at different times in history, both distinguished mechanical catechetical questioning from Socratic questioning. They recommended the latter to stimulate reasoning and personal understanding.

MEDICINE

During the Renaissance, the Socratic Method was adapted to teaching clinical medicine by Giovanni Battista Monte (1498–1551), who taught in Padua in Italy. Later in The Netherlands, Franciscus Sylvius (1614–1672) and Herman Boerhaave (1668–1738) also maieutically questioned students (in Latin) at the bedside. The ill-structured problem was the illness of the patient. From the students, the doctor elicited the observations of the symptoms, began the process of analysis and evaluation, considered alternative interpretations, and determined the correct diagnosis. A solution was needed. The students learned to think through medical problems.

Although maieutic questioning (see Chapter 3) was not followed in medical education everywhere, it nonetheless became recognized as best practice. In the early 19th century, we read how the surgeon George James Guthrie

> in instructing his alumni [sic], adopts the "Socratic Method," as being the most likely to arrest the attention and impress the memory of the juvenile student; and he often succeeds in eliciting all the symptoms and causes, and even the diagnosis of a disease, from the answers of the young respondents. ("Examination of James Madden," 1833, p. 670)

The best clinical teachers taught Socratically (sometimes mercilessly so). Socrates did not study medicine, and we know he became frustrated and impatient about the speculations regarding nature; he turned his mind to moral problems instead. But one of the oldest adaptations of his strategy of maieutic questioning is in guiding critical thinking regarding illness.

HUMANITIES AND SCIENCES IN HIGH SCHOOL AND COLLEGE

Isaac Watts (1743), who was classically educated, recommended the Socratic Method as an effective means of teaching in general. University-educated teachers who had read selected works of Plato and Xenophon were prepared to adapt the method to their teaching practice. In the 19th century, Socratic questioning was practiced in diverse subjects at Rugby School, a prestigious British private school reshaped by Thomas Arnold and thereafter a model for Victorian elite private education. With the widening of instruction in botany and zoology, the practice of teaching close observation through questions and then drawing generalizations from the students became more common. Not so ill-structured, the problem in these cases was the perception and understanding of plants and animals. It was recognized that such questioning within empirical-inductive subjects promoted the scientific reasoning advocated by Francis Bacon.

For the college-educated, the Socratic Method became a possible means for teaching science. Close observation of an object or natural phenomenon, guided by questions, as a stimulus for scientific reasoning became part of the accepted repertoire of Socratic teaching. Indeed, this scientific adaptation would exercise a decisive influence on the development of the Socratic Method in law. Later, when Sir John Adams (1904) wrote a chapter on the Socratic Method in his primer on teaching, two of his three model Socratic dialogues actually were maieutic object lessons in science—one on insects, the other on breath. In this way, the dialogues contrasted to the conversations of Socrates, which focus on abstract concepts.

At times, university professors suggested the Socratic Method for general use in primary and secondary education (Schaeffer, 1896; Tyler, 1859, 1867). The practice of scholastic recitation, or learning by repetition from a textbook or lecture, opened a space within the classroom routine that might be used for Socratic questioning. Although originally progressive in intention, many recitations hardened into for-mulaic experiences, with the student repeating the language from the textbook for a teacher who had, at most, a high school diploma (Cuban, 1993). McLellan and Dewey's (1890) text in particular gives examples of Socratic sequences of questions in geometry, grammar, and arithmetic. It was recognized that Socratic questioning stimulated thinking, challenging the student to reason and reorganize his or her knowledge (Bode, 1927; Thayer, 1928).

PROFESSIONAL EDUCATION: THE LAW AND BUSINESS

Considering the study of the law to be scientific and taking inspiration from the application of the Socratic Method to the natural sciences, Christopher Columbus Langdell adapted the Socratic Method to teaching law at Harvard University in the 1870s. This adaptation was a paradigm shift in legal and professional education, and its effects are still powerfully felt (Coquillette & Kimball, 2015; Kimball, 2009). The ill-structured problems in this adaptation were problems of legal reasoning and interpretation. The aim was to train informed critical thinking in the law. By examining sequences of appellate cases through Socratic questioning of the students, Langdell moved legal education away from lecturing or apprenticeship. We will examine the legal adaptation more in Chapter 4.

The case method, used in tandem with Socratically led discussions, has been adapted to other domains of professional education. In the 1920s, again at Harvard, whose Business School dean had been educated in the law school, business schools began to use ill-structured and complex business problems, adapting the Socratic Method in discussion (Christensen, Garvin, & Sweet, 1991; Donham, 1922).

GENERAL CRITICAL THINKING

Paul and Elder (2007a, 2007b) incisively and clearly presented selected elements of the Socratic Method within the philosophical tradition of critical thinking—that is, removed from a specific domain of knowledge. They did not review how Socrates questioned within the dialogues of Plato and Xenophon. Instead, they isolated categories of reasoning (e.g., purpose, information, concepts, assumptions, consequences, implications) and composed corresponding question prompts. There is the clear understanding that each category of reasoning generates a distinctive form of thinking. Paul (2005) has written some of the most accessible texts on critical thinking. What is consciously missing from his works is the adaptation of Socratic questioning to domains, selecting or emphasizing elements according to the demands of the domain. Paul's work also does not contain leading questions, a distinctive feature of Socratic examination in the dialogues.

STRATEGIES FOR LARGE GROUPS:
COLD-CALLING AND CONDUCTING

Group size also influences the adaptation of the Socratic Method. Socrates systematically questioned individuals; he did not moderate discussions, nor step back and observe the discussions of others. But the exigencies of the modern classroom, which may have large groups of students, have led to the development of strategies to encourage preparation and participation. Some of the strategies are authoritarian, others democratic, and still others laissez-faire.

One older, authoritarian, and often unwelcome strategy is cold-calling, or calling randomly on individual students within the large class. Proponents of cold-calling feel that the possibility of a student being called upon before his or her peers motivates conscientious and regular preparation. The strategy also allows the teacher to control the discussion, so that a few talkative students do not dominate (Warren, 1942). Whereas Socrates began his discussions by eliciting the intuitive convictions of others (i.e., no immediate preparation was required), students within the modern classroom are accountable for detailed knowledge and understanding of their assignments. They must know determined facts, concepts, principles, and methodologies. Most students do not want to be caught unprepared and embarrassed before their peers, even without a haranguing from the teacher. Although some might argue for its effectiveness, cold-calling instills a nervous, uncertain tone that many teachers (myself included) wish to avoid. Obviously Socrates did not cold-call in the Agora.

Another strategy—usually more democratic and pleasant in nature—is to become the "orchestra conductor." In the same manner that a conductor directs the sections of the orchestra, bringing the string, woodwind, brass, and percussion sections into a harmonious performance, so the Socratic discussion conductor appeals to the different students of the class for a cooperative discussion. This strategy seems to have a kind of precedent in the dialogues by Plato and Xenophon, for different speakers will have different points of view, and Socrates explores each view with the speaker before the group. For example, in the first book of *The Republic*, Socrates examines different ideas of justice before those gathered in the house of Polemarchus. Old Cephalus has one idea, his son Polemarchus another, and the irascible Thrasymachus yet another. For the Socratic conductor, participation may be democratically elicited, a strategy that is feasible if the students have demonstrated themselves to be regularly prepared and engaged. The teacher requests the participation of the students, thus avoiding the stress of cold-calling. Voluntary participation lends a more relaxed and less inquisitorial tone to the discussion.

Ideally, with prepared and engaged students, the Socratic dialogues become laissez-faire, but not in the sense of license and anarchy. Rather, everyone becomes Socrates. For instance, diverse participants suggest counterexamples and hypotheticals. Although the dialogues by Xenophon and Plato are literary works that, in part, serve to exonerate and commemorate Socrates, it is known that those who gathered around him assimilated his method or strategy of questioning. They learned how to think through questioning, and therefore the discussions among them became lively and deft. Rather than having one person conduct the discussion in the classroom, trained and knowledgeable thinkers can improvise knowingly as jazz musicians can.

SOCRATIC IN WHAT WAY?
SOCRATIC TO WHAT EXTENT?

When someone speaks of the Socratic Method in the classroom, most often he or she is referring to an adaptation that stimulates and guides critical thinking of students within a domain. Most variations retain Socratic ignorance and refrain from making positive statements (a common temptation is to clarify or expand on student answers, rather than to seek clarification through questions). There is a reliance on asking questions. Beyond these similarities, however, there can be great divergences among the adaptations. Keeping in mind the characteristics manifested in Xenophon and Plato, one can better understand any adaptation by asking: *In what way and to what extent is it Socratic?*

Each adaptation is contextualized to a domain. Each domain focuses on different kinds of problems that require different kinds of thinking. For Socrates, the domain was moral philosophy, and his problems were the definitions of moral concepts and reasoning about moral concepts (e.g., What is virtue? What is courage? What is temperance?). Other domains have other problems and other ways of thinking about these problems. The adaptation of the Socratic Method will therefore vary.

For the Socratic teacher, the first step will often be the selection of a complex problem or, more likely, a series of complex problems that can be covered within a class period or unit. The sequence or interplay of questions, guiding the reasoning, will be contextualized to the problems as well as to the students. Socrates inductively examined definition after definition; the modern Socratic teacher may proceed by concepts as well (Wilberding, 2014). Within adaptations, teachers inductively organize problems, selecting and arranging problem after problem, case after case, patient after patient, dilemma after dilemma, and text after text. These problems activate student thinking.

Comprehension of the problem is the first phase of the class discussion. This may presuppose a degree of content knowledge in student (keep in mind that the Socratic Method is not intended for delivering information). Probing this knowledge will become part of the discussion. Twenty-four centuries ago, walking through the Agora, Socrates did not ask content or fact questions of this kind. But today, if one is to be competent as a computer scientist, historian, biologist, doctor, lawyer, or businessperson, one must have mastered the basic knowledge and skills. Therefore, questions that require memorization of a corpus of knowledge are commonly interspersed in Socratic sequences. Such content must inform competent analysis and judgment.

Once students understand the problem, the teacher may begin a sequence of questions that extend analysis and judgment. A single question is not Socratic; to respond to a student's question by asking him or her that same question is not Socratic. Socrates asked sequences of questions that guided others to new insight. Recalling Bloom's (1956) taxonomy, the teacher's sequence may help a student move from simple memory recall to personal understanding, or from personal understanding to application. Further questions from the teacher focus on the higher level reasoning of analysis and evaluation. All of these questions can intermingle— that is, a sequence of questions may appeal to memory and understanding as well as personal analysis and evaluation.

In adaptations, some distinctively Socratic elements are removed completely. For instance, most adaptations abandon leading questions altogether, as they can stifle and inhibit free expression and interaction. A class period of 60 minutes filled with leading questions is unimaginable; student expression and interaction deserve greater freedom. Yet it is impossible to imagine a Socratic dialogue by Xenophon or Plato without leading questions, which are a central element. Socrates used leading questions to introduce one discrete idea after another; a series of agreements between Socrates and the other person then led to a conclusion. There may be moments in the contemporary classroom in which leading questions are helpful. For instance, Warren (1942) recommended using a logical series of yes and no questions to think through a thorny legal problem. For him, the leading question permitted rigorous and precise reasoning. For other reasons, Herbert (1652), like the Brothers of the Christian Schools (1912), recommended using leading questions only with weaker students. Most adaptations do not use them at all.

In the contemporary classroom, we can observe adaptations of the Socratic Method (see Figure 3). As domains of knowledge have proliferated over the years, and as the nature and dynamics of classroom teaching have developed, there have been modifications to stimulate and guide the critical thinking necessary for the

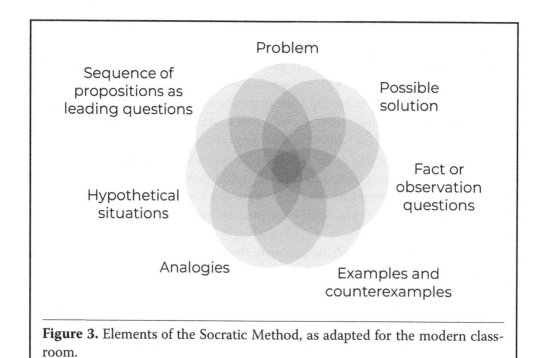

Figure 3. Elements of the Socratic Method, as adapted for the modern classroom.

array of subjects in schools. Today there is a spectrum of Socratic Methods, from the very loose adaptation of Socratic Circles to the highly rigorous adaptation in law schools. Teachers who are aware of the variations have more choices and strategies to enrich their classroom practice.

CHAPTER 3

MAIEUTIC QUESTIONING

RENAISSANCE PROBLEM SOLVING IN SCIENCE AND MEDICINE

The Socratic Method has been pursued with brilliant success by some of the greatest clinical teachers who have ever lived. It has received its highest development at the hands of physicians, and is capable of being made a most efficient instrument for conveying lessons which sink deep into the mind. . . .

—*The British Medical Journal* (1886, p. 353)

MAIEUTIC (MIDWIFE) QUESTIONING

The word *maieutic* is derived from the Greek word *maya*, which means "midwife." In Plato's *Theaetetus*, a dialogue that attempts to define what knowledge is, Socrates describes himself as a midwife of the mind. Socrates's mother had become a midwife following the death of his father. Midwives, he explains, can discern whether a woman is pregnant or not, can induce the pains of labor or reduce them, can cause childbirth, and, if necessary, can promote a miscarriage. From their experience, they can even astutely suggest which couples will produce the best children.

DOI: 10.4324/9781003238089-4

Through his questioning, Socrates explains, he assists souls in delivering ideas. His midwifery of the soul is even more difficult than general midwifery because it is challenging to distinguish an error from a truth. Maieutic questioning (in the past sometimes called *obstetric questioning*) is midwife questioning. The questioner helps the other person give birth to his or her ideas.

MAIEUTIC PASSAGES IN PLATO'S DIALOGUES

▸ *Theaetetus* (148e–151d): Socrates explains how he is a midwife of the mind.

▸ *Meno* (82c–85c): Socrates assists a slave boy in solving a problem in geometry.

▸ *Euthydemus* (278c–282d): Socrates helps Clinias understand that, to become happy, one must pursue wisdom and learn philosophy.

▸ *Euthydemus* (288d–290d): Socrates leads Clinias to understand how the knowledge of both making and wisely using renders one happy.

▸ *Protagoras* (310b–314d): Socrates guides Hippocrates to consider what he expects to learn from the sophist Protagoras.

Socrates helps others "discover a multitude of beautiful things, which they bring forth into the light" (Plato, *Theaetetus*, 150d). In the succeeding centuries, this more constructive approach to questioning has become known as maieutic questioning.

Socrates had a gift for finding examples and metaphors from common occupations. The metaphor of the midwife expresses many aspects of the experience of questioning. In early dialogues, Socrates may be portrayed as a more assertive inquisitor. Euthyphro and others learn that their definitions are inadequate, but do not arrive at a positive answer. The role of the midwife, which clearly does not preclude the possibility of pain in birth, has often been interpreted as a gentler and less frustrating guide to learning. Maieutic questioning leads to a correct answer, not simply to a person's realization that he or she does not know the answer.

To look briefly at an example, within *Meno*, Socrates assists a slave boy in finding the solution to a problem of geometry (how to double the area of a square that measures 2 x 2) through maieutic questioning. For Plato, this examples demonstrates a theory of innate knowledge and recollection. Leaving that to one side, we see Socrates questioning the boy and leading him through the logical consequences of his assumptions. First, the boy believes that simply by doubling the length and width of a square, one obtains the doubling of the area of the square. But Socrates guides the reasoning, and they come to the realization that this would quadruple the area: A square of 2 x 2 has an area of 4, whereas a square of 4 x 4 has an area of 16. They need a square whose area is 8. They next follow the boy's intuition that the length and width must be 3, but this cannot be true either, for they obtain a square whose area is 9. At this juncture, Socrates points out that the slave boy now realizes that he does not know, and this stimulates greater interest in finding the solution to the problem. Dissipating the illusory feeling of knowing is an important phase in maieutic questioning. Then, Socrates questions the boy further, and the two draw four equal squares of 2 x 2 in the configuration of a large square of 4 x 4. Then, the two find the diagonals of the smaller squares, and thus a square that is double the area of 2 x 2 appears within the center of the larger square of 4 x 4. By using the diagonal of 2 x 2 as the length and width, one obtains the doubling of the area of the 2 x 2 square.

Socrates uses leading questions, for the most part, in guiding the slave boy to reason from his assumptions. It is noteworthy that mistakes are an important part of the learning process. The slave boy discovers that his first two hypotheses were wrong. Discovering incorrect answers is important because is permits the realization that one does not know. From this awareness, curiosity grows. Then, one can build more methodically with an attitude of skepticism. One understands that one must guess and test.

A PARADIGM SHIFT: FROM PHILOSOPHY TO NATURAL SCIENCE

Cicero praised Socrates for taking philosophy from the heavens and bringing it to Earth. He believed that Socrates directed philosophical reasoning away from the inconclusive speculations on natural phenomena of the Pre-Socratics and focused it principally upon ethical and political questions. The question was not "What is life?" but "What is the good life?" Although Socrates may have used natural phenomena in analogies (e.g., bees, wax, the sun), he never directed attention and critical reasoning to natural phenomena in themselves to understand a chain of causes. He did not seek to investigate, model, and explain natural phenomena. Nonetheless, since the Renaissance, his method of questioning has, at times and in different ways, been redirected to teaching science.

Science has become the dominant paradigm for trustworthy knowledge. Since the 19th century, it has increasingly moved into the center of the curriculum.

Science, technology, engineering, and mathematics are interdependent domains in which rapid change is characteristic. Recently the Next Generation Science Standards (NGSS Lead States, 2013) sought ambitiously and meticulously to redesign comprehensive science education. In addition to its focus on mastering disciplinary practices and core ideas, the NGSS outlined an array of important critical thinking practices. Among other practices, students must be able to distinguish a scientific (or testable) question from a nonscientific (or untestable) question, discern the premises and evidence within an argument, differentiate causation and correlation, discuss the limitations of a model, develop a hypothesis based on a model or theory, plan an experiment or field research, analyze data, and evaluate the strength of a conclusion (National Research Council, 2012). The Socratic Method may be used to teach all of these practices.

Maieutic questioning, which may scaffold reasoning in different ways, is the most versatile form of the Socratic Method, for it can be adapted to learning these critical thinking skills (or practices, as the NGSS distinguishes) in problem solving. It effectively guides reasoning through more open problems.

Many are familiar with the gradual release of responsibility model of instruction, perhaps better known as *I Do, We Do, You Do*, articulated by Pearson and Gallagher (1983). The model includes five phases (Duke, Pearson, Strachan, & Billman, 2011). First, the teacher engages in direct instruction, describing the practice or skill and how it should be used. Next, the teacher and/or a student models the skill, thinking aloud (I Do). Thirdly, there is a phase of shared responsibility with collaborative use of the skill, and then, fourthly, guided practice (We Do). In the third and fourth phases, there is a gradual release of responsibility, with the teacher stepping back as the student grasps the skill more securely. Then, in the fifth and final phase, the student practices the skill autonomously (You Do). Maieutic questioning is a Socratic form of *We Do* in a continuum of the gradual release of responsibility.

Often blending with dialogue and debate, maieutic questioning has been adapted to the teaching of natural science and medicine. As stated in the previous chapter, the pattern and content of Socratic questioning necessarily change with a change of domain and way of thinking. There are new emphases in how questioning accompanies rigorous reasoning and judgment. Within the paradigm of science, the pattern of the Socratic Method shifts. We can therefore ask the following: What kinds of questions are distinctively scientific questions? How is scientific reasoning about these questions distinctive? How can maieutic questioning and Socratic dialogue be inserted in teaching science?

SOCRATIC QUESTIONING FOR SCIENTIFIC PROBLEMS

Science offers a surprising and counterintuitive understanding of the workings of nature (Wolpert, 1992). It appears to be the critical thinking subject par excellence; one needs to reason very well to understand many of the truths we learn in school. The simple question "Why are there four seasons?" can stump the average person. Yet, within the NGSS, this topic is covered in middle school Earth and space science (Disciplinary Core Idea ESS1.B; NGSS Lead States, 2013). Intuitively, the Earth does not appear round; we do not easily perceive its curvature. Yet, through careful observation, measurement, and reasoning, Eratosthenes calculated its circumference in the third century BCE. Aristarchus, and later Copernicus, suggested the heliocentric theory in the same manner. The 23-degree of tilt of the Earth was measured in ancient China, India, and Greece, but more accurately by Tycho Brahe. Kepler calculated the laws of planetary motion in ellipses. Bringing these measurements and discoveries together, a person can reason that when the Northern Hemisphere of the tilted Earth in its elliptical orbit receives more sun, it is summer; when it receives less sun, it is winter. The solstices mark the beginning and end of these periods. During the Northern Hemisphere's winter, the rays of the sun strike the Southern Hemisphere more directly, and so it is summer there; when the Southern Hemisphere is tilted away, it is winter. These empirical explanations are discovered through careful observation, measurement, and reasoning. Such truths are not held in place by an authority; they are not relative to a person or organization. Anyone can understand the steps in reasoning from observations and measurements that can be verified. This empirical-inductive reasoning, first extolled by Francis Bacon and René Descartes, is characteristic of many sciences (Conant, 1964).

Traditionally the process is presented as broadly linear, but the reality of practicing science is more fluid and dynamic (Understanding Science, n.d.). It quite perfectly represents the paradigm of constructed knowledge about which King and Kitchener (2002) wrote. The process of discovering new ideas takes into account an exploration of the existing scientific literature and the viva voce sharing of ideas within the community of scientists, who most often work in teams rather than in isolation (as demonstrated in the four seasons example). This process leads to the testing of ideas through the gathering and interpreting of data. This interpretation is then critically reviewed by the larger community of scientists and contributes to the building of knowledge, the development of technology, and the informing of policy, among other goals.

Formulated on the basis of evidence and reasoning, a theory in science is an explanation with predictive power. Such a theory is continually open to modification or rejection, for science operates by falsification (i.e., by attempting to prove its theories false, not by confirming them). Skepticism is a powerful and necessary attitude in scientific thinking. Theories are expected to be modified, as has happened continually in the history of science, as we move to a more accurate understanding of nature. A theory that cannot be proven false through empirical evidence and reasoning is not scientific. Other domains of knowledge may have other forms of evidence. Pseudosciences may purport to make claims similar to scientific claims, but their evidence is not empirical, their reasoning may be flawed, and their theories cannot be falsified.

However, not all questions are scientific questions. Which form of government is best? Does God exist? Is it always just to follow the law? How can human beings be happy? Why did World War I begin? Did Moses exist? There are many fundamentally important questions that the scientific method cannot address—or its use will be more limited, particularly in the realm of values (although there are dissenters on this point).

A scientific question attempts to answer how an aspect of nature works. It should be an empirical question. From that point, a hypothesis that is falsifiable can be formed, and a prediction made. As Medawar (1996) wrote in more analytical language, a "hypothesis is an imaginative preconception of what might be true in the form of a declaration with verifiable deductive consequences" (p. 18). Then, an experiment or investigation appropriate for testing the hypothesis can be designed. Within the experiment, variables are consciously controlled for the gathering of relevant data. Data are collected and analyzed, and a conclusion can be drawn. The hypothesis will then be accepted, modified, or discarded. This is the *hypothetico-deductive method*.

Maieutic questioning and dialogue can be inserted in several stages while conducting science lessons. For instance, dialogue can be used to develop student skills in observation to perceive more accurately. Socratic questioning can also assist students in developing questions and problems that can be tested and solved. It can guide analysis and interpretation of data to detect or challenge patterns or trends. Socratic questions can guide student analysis in mathematics and computational thinking. More broadly, teachers can maieutically question within a Socratic discussion on the nature of science, through activities or texts that express how science is different from pseudoscience or nonscience.

Let us first look at what is meant by *maieutic questioning*.

MAIEUTIC OBSERVATION, ANALYSIS, AND EVALUATION IN MEDICINE

In the early modern period, although the Socratic Method continued to be used in theological polemics, it surfaced within the teaching of clinical medicine—that is, with the practical training of students in the observation of symptoms and the inductive formulation of a diagnosis at the bedside of the patient. In this adaptation, some aspects of the ancient Socratic Method are removed and others are emphasized. In a sense, the example of clinical medicine bridges practices, for one must not only explain a phenomenon (the illness), but also find a solution (the cure). (*Note.* Within its eight practices, the NGSS distinguishes the construction of explanations in science from the designing of solutions in engineering.) According to Socrates, a person cannot claim that his sole fragment of knowledge is that *he knows that he does not know*. On the contrary, he must have a reasonable solution within an evidence-based theory. We must keep in mind that a significant degree of content knowledge is taken for granted. The Socratic Method is used to develop reasoning, not to impart information.

This Renaissance adaptation, which can be transposed to secondary education, has many advantages. It permits an informed and open analysis and evaluation by the students. The teacher intercedes and guides the students through maieutic questioning if they lose their path during analysis and evaluation. Clearly, such a classroom discussion cannot simply include the sharing of subjective opinions among the students, for there need to be accurate analysis and correct judgment. Today the decision-making process in diagnosis is more complex, as doctors must take into account a wealth of details, including the history of the patient, physical examination, laboratory findings, and imaging. Socratic questioning, however, is still used in teaching clinical medicine, although it has different interpretations and can be undertaken with different tones.

The appearance of the Socratic Method in medicine is a very early and remarkable example of problem-based learning. In the 17th century, a Dutch doctor, Franz de le Boë, known also Franciscus Sylvius, described his method of teaching students at the bedside of patients in Saint Caecilia hospital in Leiden:

> I have led my pupils by the hand into medical practice, using a method unknown at Leyden, or perhaps elsewhere; that is, taking them daily to visit the sick at the public hospital. There I have put the symptoms of disease before their eyes; have let them hear the complaints of the patients and have asked them their opinions as to the causes and rational treatment of each case. Whenever dif-

ferences of opinion arose among them concerning these things, I, in a quiet way, pitted against each other those holding different opinions, in order that they might mutually satisfy themselves by examining all aspects of the matter, finally giving my own judgment regarding the various views. With me they confirmed the happy results of the treatment, if God rewarded our labours by the return to health of the patients, or assisted in the examination of the cadaver when the patients finally paid the inevitable tribute of death. (Jones, 1952, p. 468)

Sylvius took credit for the innovation, but in the late Renaissance, this Socratic practice arose first in Padua, Italy, and students brought it to The Netherlands (Hull, 1997; Withington, 1894).

A pupil of Sylvius recalled:

When he came with his pupils to the patient and began to teach, he appeared completely in the dark as to the causes or the nature of the affection the patient was suffering from, and at first expressed no opinion upon the case; he then began by questions put to different members of his audience to fish out everything and finally united the facts discovered in this manner into a complete picture of the disease in such a way that the students received the impression that they had themselves made the diagnosis and not learnt it from him. (Parent, 2016, p. 597)

The precise sequence of interaction, sentence by sentence within the conversation, cannot be known. But the Socratic characteristics are striking, as are the divergences from the Socratic Method. We can see how at first the problem was collectively defined, and then the solution collectively sought. During the problem/solution investigation, the teacher questioned as necessary within student dialogue and debate (as we will see later with the legal adaptation).

The illness itself was a question in need of clarification and identification; a diagnosis had to be made before a treatment could be prescribed. Sylvius (Jones, 1952) displayed Socratic ignorance in affecting not to understand the illness before him. It fell upon the students to analyze a real-life problem through empirical-inductive inquiry. They had to define the problem on the basis of what they saw and what the patient said. Sylvius asked their opinions but also questioned them to bring out the specific details. He would maieutically "fish out" all of these details by asking questions to different members of the group ("Examination of James Madden," 1833, p. 670). Maieutic questioning, representing the *We Do* phase of the gradual release of responsibility model (Pearson & Gallagher, 1983), kept the students focused on the correct symptoms. Then, they could deduce an accurate diagnosis.

Often we see a dichotomy asserted between dialogue and debate, with the latter activity taking on a negative connotation for its competitiveness. On the one hand, an organized debate in parliamentary style will not resemble a conversation, for the structure will permit only argument and rebuttal in turns. On the other hand, a conversation negotiating a polite conflict of reasoned and evidence-based viewpoints is an important analytical activity that allows for civil discourse. In medicine, dialogue and debate mix as students clarify symptoms, the identity of the illness, its causes, and its treatment. Sylvius conducted a group discussion in this more democratic manner (Jones, 1952). In this way, he found the dialectic within the students.

This kind of Socratic questioning does not appear within the ancient dialogues. Nonetheless, it is an effective strategy for enlivening the group analysis and evaluation. Rather than encourage constant teacher-student interaction, Sylvius quietly directed the students to respond to each other (Jones, 1952). The analysis thus became a collective activity. By not placing a single student under intensive scrutiny, as in the traditional recitation, Sylvius enabled the entire group. The discussion took place in Latin, so many patients were mercifully oblivious to its possibly alarming content. Sylvius listened nonjudgmentally and did not pounce on incorrect answers. The students worked out the solution, and he intervened as necessary.

The Renaissance pedagogical conversation within the group had the loose and effective format portrayed in Figure 4. Sylvius's Socratic restraint lasted until the end of the exploration, when he gave his own judgment of the expressed views and then confirmed or provided the correct diagnosis. The students actively and successfully assimilated a process of clinical reasoning and judgment. Clearly, arriving at a solution at the end of the conversation is not a Socratic element either. But, in medicine, a student or doctor seeks the correct interpretation within a theory based on evidence and rigorous reasoning. Unlike in an open, philosophical discussion, which might not result in a definitive and satisfactory answer, in medicine, the recovery of health signaled a correct interpretation of illness and therapy.

There has been more than one interpretation of how the Socratic Method may be applied for training in clinical judgment. Sylvius's discussions were more democratic, involving the entire group in open dialogue and debate—something we will see again within the legal adaptation (see Chapter 4), as well as in Michael Sandel's (2009) practice (see Chapter 7). But a later medical adaptation, which more closely resembled a traditional 19th-century recitation, focused on sternly and rigorously examining an individual student's knowledge about a patient's condition and the proper diagnosis:

> [The student] is then questioned, and his answers form the basis
> of the instruction conveyed to his fellows. If his answers be cor-

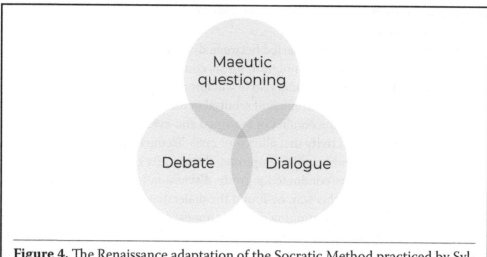

Figure 4. The Renaissance adaptation of the Socratic Method practiced by Sylvius (Jones, 1952).

rect and his conclusions just, the teacher amplifies and emphasizes them. If he has hastily rushed to a premature conclusion, a series of careful questions leads him gradually to see the inadequacy of the grounds upon which it has been based. If he has overlooked any symptom, the interrogations are so framed as to direct his attention to the affected organ, and induce him to note the symptom himself, rather than announce it plainly to him. ("The Socratic Method in Clinical Teaching," 1888, p. 834)

In this example, the other students benefit from the student's knowledge as well as from his mistakes. We see, too, the still common (and un-Socratic) practice of expanding on the student's response. For Sylvius, this method was particularly valuable when more reasoning was required, but it had a drawback, depending on who was questioning; a weak and unprepared student would have to withstand "the full battery of interrogation and sarcasm from a man of long experience and ample information, who easily forgets that he was once as raw and ignorant as his helpless victim" ("The Socratic Method in Clinical Teaching," 1888, p. 834). More than 100 years later, this more hostile, adversarial questioning, strangely but commonly called "pimping," which is clearly counterproductive and not part of Socratic practice, is still encountered in clinical education and has generated considerable criticism in recent years (Brancati, 1989; Carlson, 2017; Kost & Chen, 2015; Reifler, 2015; Stoddard & O'Dell, 2016; Wear, Kokinova, Keck-McNulty, & Aultman, 2005).

THE VERSATILITY OF MAIEUTIC QUESTIONING

As it always takes place within a structure of gradual release from responsibility, maieutic questioning may have various applications and differing degrees of direction. It is best used at the discretion of the teacher in response to a discovered difficulty experienced by the learner or group of learners. It may also play a part in the teaching of interconnecting practices, processes, and skills. Pólya (2014) wisely suggested beginning with general questions before posing more specific ones. In other words, the teacher does not start with the highly articulated sequence of leading questions, but instead challenges the student to the degree necessary to permit more autonomous thinking.

More restrained and general maieutic questioning permits a more open and nondirective analysis and evaluation by the students. Seeing something overlooked and unmentioned, or something out of focus, the instructor can step in and "fish out" or focus the details as necessary within an analytical conversation among the students. This fishing out can be happen at any stage within the structure or methodology of problem solving. It can be adapted to the teaching of interconnecting practices and skills. In the activity of observation, for example, in which understanding informs and defines what one perceives, maieutic questioning can guide the recognition of overlooked significant details. We commonly think that "seeing is believing," but it is equally true that "believing is seeing," as our understanding determines what we perceive (Abel, 1976). We see selectively.

At the other pole of maieutic questioning is the more explicit, directive questioning used to guide someone toward a valid conclusion. As Socrates questions the slave boy in Plato's *Meno*, he assists the development of the boy's reasoning from an intuition, assumption, or premise to its logical conclusion. Socrates uses specific leading questions to articulate explicitly the inferences step by step. Incorrect intuitions, assumptions, or premises lead to incorrect conclusions. The process of working through incorrect answers is itself instructive. Within other dialogues (e.g., *Euthydemus*), Socrates works out the reasoning step by step to guide someone to a valid and insightful conclusion. In the same way, when students encounter difficulties in understanding during Socratic sequences, teachers can give them choices, thereby scaffolding more active thinking.

In addition to these two manifestations, maieutic questioning can also pose general questions that focus the phases of solving a problem. In Pólya's (1963) schema, the four general steps are (1) understanding the problem, (2) devising a plan, (3) carrying out the plan, and (4) looking back. Each of these steps contains further maieutic questions, which can be rephrased, to direct the student's atten-

49

tion to aspects of the problem and, through repetition in solving different problems, to inculcate the strategy of problem solving.

DIALOGUE AND DEBATE:
PROBLEM, SOLUTION, PROBE, REVIEW

The Renaissance variation of the Socratic Method is based on a problem for discussion and debate. A teacher, therefore, first selects a problem and broadly organizes the discussion with content and exploratory questions. Within the discussion, at any point when there is not consensus, the teacher must deftly choreograph a debate, asking the students to explain aloud what they think and why they think this. The teacher asks them how they can distinguish which belief is more justified. Maieutic questioning intercedes when students are baffled and cannot see their way to the correct understanding.

THE RENAISSANCE VARIATION
Steps

1. Select a problem.

2. Draft the content and exploratory questions.

3. Prepare the maieutic sequence for key details or concepts.

4. Prepare a choice of extension activities.

What if there is no debate? Generally speaking, there is often a variety of viewpoints within the classroom; usually the real issue is how comfortable the students are in expressing their views. An authoritarian classroom is a silent (and often bored) classroom. However, teachers can also suggest alternative points of view and ask students to reason through them, thereby sparking debate (see Table 1 for questions to consider during this process).

TABLE 1
Maieutic Questioning: Problem, Solution, Probe, Review

Problem	▸ What is the problem here? ▸ What has happened here? ▸ Why do you think this? ▸ Is there a part of the problem you do not understand? ▸ Have you seen a problem like this before? ▸ Do you know an analogous problem? ▸ Is this similar to another problem? ▸ What are other possibilities for the problem? ▸ What would the term be for this?
Solution	▸ What is your solution? ▸ What makes you think this? ▸ Can you explain your reasoning? ▸ Can you clarify . . . ? ▸ Why do you think that . . . ? ▸ What led you to your conclusion? ▸ How do you interpret . . . ? ▸ What evidence is there to support your conclusion? ▸ In your own words, how would you . . . ?
Probe	▸ What would be an alternative point of view? Why is your judgment better than this alternative? ▸ How did you eliminate the possibility that . . . ? ▸ How does this compare with . . . ? ▸ Do you think this is similar to . . . ? ▸ How does this contrast with . . . ? ▸ Can you link this to . . . ? ▸ What assumption are you making when you say . . . ? ▸ What is the basis for your judgment that . . . ? ▸ How can you check the solution? ▸ Distinguish . . . ▸ Suppose . . . ▸ What if . . . ? ▸ What consequence would there be if . . . ? ▸ What implication is there if . . . ? ▸ Predict . . . ▸ What plan would you make . . . ?
Review	*Review the correct points. Provide specific feedback on student arguments.*

DEVELOPING PRACTICES, HABITS, AND JUDGMENT

As discovered in Renaissance, when natural science began to calve off from philosophy, maieutic questioning was a possible means for instruction in observation and reasoning—that is, in the empirical-inductive method of creating knowledge in science. The teacher started with problems, and the problems were natural phenomena (illnesses). Within a group dialogue and debate, the teacher guided the students in the close observation of significant characteristics and then to a correct generalization or conclusion.

In the 19th century, this approach was applied to the teaching of botany (Wilson, 1867). In the first lesson, the teacher gave secondary students a plant specimen. Through the guidance of the teacher's questions, the students proceeded to dissect the specimen, learning the individual parts but not the names. In the next lessons, the students repeated the same process with two other plants, gradually generating personal comparison and contrast, as well as the drawing of generalizations and classification. The process was similar to Hilda Taba's simple and effective question sequences of listing, grouping, and labeling to develop generalizations (Durkin, 1993). This maieutic questioning could take place with specimens in the classroom, within the laboratory, or outside in nature.

Maieutic questioning can be transposed from individuals to groups. In this way, the teacher leads a collective inquiry into alternative points of view or arguments, guiding the examination of evidence and reasoning. The early adaptation of the Socratic Method to medicine is revealing for its fusion of theoretical and practical knowledge. The doctor must reason actively with each patient. One major difference from Socrates's questioning is that the maieutic questioning takes place within a context that require rigorous mastery of a body of learning. Both teacher and student must be in command of basic content and more nuanced understandings as well.

Within medical education, *precepting* is the personal clinical training and evaluation of doctor or nurse. Maieutic questioning remains in place among a gamut of variations for precepting (e.g., One-Minute Preceptor, SNAPPS), used to foster the development of accurate clinical judgment (Cunningham, Blatt, Fuller, & Weinberger, 1999; Neher, Gordon, Meyer, & Stevens, 1992; Wolpaw, Wolpaw, & Papp, 2003). This latest adaptation or development of the Socratic Method includes a review of the facts and the possible diagnoses, as well as a probing of the pros and cons of the possible diagnoses to eliminate the less likely ones. It also encourages doctors and nurses to reinforce accurate understandings and clearly correct misunderstandings.

Maieutic questioning patiently instills a thinking routine in approaching ill-structured, real-life problems. In the well-known formulation, *I Do, We Do, You Do*, maieutic questioning begins with *We Do* and guides the students to *You Do*. There is a gradual release from responsibility as the students become more autonomous in their understanding and practice. By suggesting, probing, and hinting, as Sylvius described Socratic practice (Jones, 1952), the teacher scaffolds the formation of logical reasoning and balanced judgment of the students ("The Socratic Method in Clinical Teaching," 1888).

CHAPTER 4

THE LEGAL ADAPTATION OF THE SOCRATIC METHOD

What is the Socratic Method, after all, but discussion designed to sow doubt in order to develop insight and understanding?

—John G. Roberts, Jr., Chief Justice of the Supreme Court

SOCRATIC TESTING OF PRINCIPLES IN THE COURTROOM AND CLASSROOM

Ill-structured problems, as King and Kitchener (2002) wrote, challenge students to reason more rigorously. One of the best-known applications of the Socratic Method, which makes ample use of ill-structured problems, is within the domain of law, both within the classroom and within the courtroom itself (Abrams, 2015; Clark, 1992; Sullivan, Colby, Wegner, Bond, & Shulman, 2007). When an appellate case is to be judged by the Supreme Court, there is a session of oral argument in which attorneys for both sides present their cases. By questioning the attorneys, the nine justices expertly probe the argument. Often the questions include hypo-

DOI: 10.4324/9781003238089-5

thetical situations to help the justices envision better the possible consequences and implications of any change in the law—both for the law itself and for society. For instance, in the highly publicized case of *Masterpiece Cakeshop v. Colorado Civil Rights Commission*, which concerned freedom of speech, freedom of religion, and freedom from discrimination, and whose argument was heard on December 5, 2017, the Supreme Court tested the arguments in this Socratic manner. The lawyer for Masterpiece Cakeshop argued that compelling a baker to create a cake whose message violated his religious beliefs was compelled speech that violated the First Amendment. The justices wished to test the idea that the cake was an act of speech. Justice Ruth Bader Ginsburg asked who else might be considered an artist whose creation constituted speech—the florist whose floral arrangement was used . . . the designer of the wedding invitation or menu? Justice Elena Kagan asked whether the jeweller, the hairstylist, the makeup artist, or the tailor were also artists demonstrating speech at the wedding. Moving beyond the wedding context, Justice Samuel Alito asked whether an architectural design would be considered protected speech. In a Mexican restaurant, would a special recipe for mole sauce be protected speech? On the petitioner's side, the Solicitor General Noel Francisco asked whether an African American sculptor could be compelled to sculpt a cross for a Ku Klux Klan service. Incisively expressed in a few words, these hypothetical situations tested a principle in terms of the person acting (the artist), the object (the artwork or artifact), the context, and the action. All of this testing was Socratic in nature.

The Socratic character of the exchanges in oral arguments becomes clearer when compared with the conversation about justice between Socrates and a bookish young man called Euthydemus in Xenophon's *Memoirs* (Book IV, Chapter 2). Euthydemus exclaims, as anyone would, that he can recognize the works of justice and distinguish them from the works of injustice. Socrates then draws two columns, marking one "J" for Justice and the other "I" for Injustice, and calmly asks Euthydemus where he would place the act of lying. Euthydemus puts it under Injustice. Socrates then asks about deceit, doing mischief, and selling a person into slavery. One by one Euthydemus places each of these acts into the column for Injustice. Then, Socrates asks where Euthydemus would place a general enslaving a hostile and unjust city, a general deceiving an enemy when at war, and a general who steals the enemy's goods. Euthydemus places all of these situations under Justice. Frustrated at the series of hypothetical situations, Euthydemus exclaims that he thought Socrates was asking how one should behave justly with one's friends. Socrates then suggests the following scenarios: a general who tells his discouraged troops that reinforcements are arriving when in reality this is not so; a son who refuses to take medicine, so his father tells him the medicine is food; and a man who takes the sword of a friend who is not in his right mind. Euthydemus claims that all of these fall under the Justice column. Confronted with different sequences of short hypothetical situations, Euthydemus realizes that the discernment of justice and injustice is no easy matter.

The Socratic Method holds a niche in many first-year law courses. The 2007 Carnegie Report on legal education noted the success of first-year programs that relied on "the case-dialogue method" (Sullivan et al., 2007). The common law system in the United States requires reasoning upon precedent, according to the principle of *stare decisis*. Applied to real-life cases, the Socratic Method offers a means for legal analysis and evaluation of complex issues, as well as the testing of rules in diverse and dissimilar circumstances (Katz & O'Neill, 2009; Schwartz, Hess, & Sparrow, 2013). Law is constructed knowledge.

Complex and subtle as it may become in professional legal education, the legal variation of the Socratic Method may be easily transposed to secondary education to challenge students to reason beyond the absolutist and authority-dependent categories of prereflective thinking (King & Kitchener, 1994, 2002). By carefully selecting or crafting a series of cases or problems, a teacher can develop and turn an issue or concept in different directions. Rather than strictly from the domain of law, cases (real or imaginary) can originate from any domain of knowledge. Teachers can use cases from science (Herreid, 2007), the arts, history, literature, ethics, religion, or mathematics. A series of parables on a single issue or theme may be understood as a series of cases. A sequence of artworks, or Fermi Problems, may become a sequence of cases. An interdisciplinary collection of cases can challenge students to think in a more holistic manner about the creation of knowledge.

One might argue that the legal variation is the first flipped classroom. The teacher assigns the cases beforehand for close study, and much essential information is communicated through preparatory readings, individual study, and perhaps group discussion. Before class begins, students are expected to understand the basic facts, the legal issue, the holding (judgment), and the rationale for the judgment. This preparation permits informed class discussion.

In addition to the selection of cases, the questioning strategy used in examining the sequence in the classroom is Socratic. Socratic questioning—when done patiently, at the proper pace, and in the right tone—deftly exploits the possibilities of problem-based, concept-oriented education. By modifying details of the problems to emphasize, reduce, or eliminate aspects of the issue or concept, the Socratic instructor guides students to acknowledge and engage with analysis and a continuum of judgments. Like Euthydemus, students must reconsider intuitive responses and reason more carefully and reflectively.

In explaining the legal variation, I would like to present its origins at Harvard Law in 1870, as well as an explanation from a Harvard Law professor of how a Socratic lesson is taught. I will isolate the Socratic aspects of the legal variation and suggest how this manner of teaching may be used in the classroom.

History of the Socratic Method in Legal Education

In 1869, Harvard University appointed 35-year-old Charles W. Eliot, a professor of analytical chemistry at MIT, to be its president. The following year Eliot hired Christopher Columbus Langdell, a lawyer from New York City, to teach law at the university's small law school at a time when lecture and textbooks dominated legal education in general (Kimball, 2009). Langdell (1871) observed that he himself had learned the law best through his own analysis of individual cases. He viewed the law as scientific. Like Eliot, Langdell believed the most effective method of teaching a science was a laboratory approach—inductive and demonstrative—that emphasized learning how to analyze and evaluate. At Harvard he introduced this new approach to legal teaching amid some controversy (Coquillette & Kimball, 2015; Kimball, 2009).

Inquiry-Based, Problem-Based, and Concept-Driven

Langdell's (1871) method of studying the law was the same empirical and inductive method a scientist might use to study the phenomena of nature (Kimball, 2009). As Langdell (1887) mentioned in a later address, given that the law was a science and must be learned from books, the library took a central position in its mastery—the same as the laboratory for chemists or physicists, the museum of natural history for zoologists, or the botanical garden for botanists. Langdell collected the most representative appellate cases for analysis and evaluation, and brought this anthology into the classroom. For each class, five or six cases were assigned (Wambaugh, 1906). Through close analysis of the cases, the class would detect and discuss the legal principles and doctrines, applying these to hypothetical problems as well. For Langdell, using the paradigm of natural science to understand his own discipline, the principles or doctrines of law were like species that have evolved over time. Individual legal cases were the specimens that express moments in that evolution. The analysis of significant specimens was the shortest and best path to mastery of the essential principles and doctrines. In this way, a learner could develop a sharper understanding of the law. Learning was not accomplished through the recording of lecture notes.

DEFINITIONS
Case, Problem, Hypothetical

For the purposes of this text, let us distinguish these three words carefully:

- A *case* refers to a real legal case that has been or will be judged in a court.

- A *problem* is an imaginary situation or case that contains several legal issues.

- A *hypothetical* is a short, imaginary problem that raises one issue.

In effect, Langdell collected the contract law equivalent of the selected specimens that permitted mastery of the basic principles and content of a natural science, such as botany or zoology (Kimball, 2009). Before coming to class, students read and studied assigned cases. For example, in order to examine the principle of mutual consent, Langdell (1871) assigned *Payne v. Cave*, a contract case from 1789. The case involved the legal nature of bidding at auction. Instead of lecturing students on the content of the decision and the reasoning of the judge, Langdell first asked a student to state the facts of the case. He then posed inductive questions to discern the logic of the judge's decision, making reference to legal precedents, as well as requiring the students to use and explain correct terminology. Students also needed to apply the principles or rules to different hypothetical situations.

The problem-based final examination reflected the classroom practice. It was not a simple memory-based exercise. Instead, the text required analysis, evaluation, and higher level thinking. Langdell's (1873) final examination consisted of 15 questions, 10 of which were short problems asking for an opinion and justification. The need to discern the issue, apply the law, and explain reasoning was paramount.

At first Langdell's efforts faltered (a fact from which all teachers can take consolation), but they improved rapidly, and soon others saw the value of his Socratic approach that emphasized the cultivation of students' critical thinking. Former students of Langdell's, such as James Barr Ames, began to teach in this manner. Ames (1874a, 1874b, 1876a, 1876b) modified Langdell's approach from chronological sequencing of cases to thematic sequencing, and his examinations also featured challenging legal problems (Williams, 1992). By the time of Langdell's death in 1906, the Langdell Method, which at times was called the inductive method, was well on its way to becoming the outstanding method of teaching the law, especially in the first year of law study (Kimball, 2009). Langdell's thick casebook, filled with hundreds of representative legal cases, increasingly became the standard legal textbook, which would acquire more materials to support student learning in the ensuing decades.

Case-based Socratic discussion can be particularly useful as a formative method, for it is inquiry-based in examining original sources; it is student-based, requiring students to do their own higher order reasoning (i.e., their own analysis and evaluation); and it is problem-based, requiring students to work through complex problems. Although competing theories of jurisprudence, as well as other methods of teaching, have evolved, the basic classroom activity of Socratically led analysis and evaluation of authentic cases retains value.

FROM FOXES TO BILLBOARDS: TRANSFERRING THE LEARNING

In 1956, Harvard professor Arthur E. Sutherland (1957) lucidly explained the conduct of the Socratic lesson. He described how students first are asked to read and prepare designated cases before class. For an illustration of a classroom discussion, Sutherland revealed the series of questions he might use for *Pierson v. Post* (1805), a case of property law regarding fox hunting. According to the case, Post, accompanied by his hunting dogs, was chasing a fox and was on the point of seizing it. By chance, Pierson came upon the fox, clearly saw that Post was hunting it, but killed the animal himself and carried it away, leaving Post furious. Post sued Pierson, and the court ruled in Post's favor. Pierson appealed, and the appellate court overturned the ruling. The appeals court found that Pierson had a legal right to keep the wild fox he killed. Mere pursuit of the wild animal was not enough to establish "occupancy."

Sutherland (1957) explained that, when using this case in the classroom, the law professor can ask a student to relate the facts: to reveal the plaintiff's view, to explain the legal issue, and to indicate and explain the decision of the judge. Thus far, the exercise in class is a standard recitation and can be understood pedagogically within the remembering and understanding categories of Bloom's (1956) taxonomy.

Then, with the facts, issues, and the decision established, the recitation can recede and Socratic questioning can begin (Sutherland, 1957). The law professor can ask the following questions:

▸ At the instant before the capture of the fox, to whom does the fox belong, and why?

- ▸ Suppose the facts were different: The first hunter caught the fox, and the second hunter took it away from him. Would the judgment be different? Why?
- ▸ Suppose the first hunter, having shot the fox and believing it dead, put it in his car and drove away, but the fox revived and jumped from the car, and the second hunter caught it. To whom does the fox belong, and why?
- ▸ Suppose the first hunter tamed the fox, taught it how to run in a circle, and showed it at country fairs, but one day the fox, abandoning the theatrical life, ran back to the forest, where the second hunter caught it. To whom does the fox belong, and why?

Having established how a professor might use the case in a classroom, Sutherland (1957) then demonstrated the relevance of the fox debate by using the analysis of a more recent, but imaginary, case. In the imaginary case, a car manufacturer wishes to launch a new car model with a clever advertising campaign. On a large number of billboards, he places striking but mysteriously unsigned advertisements with the message, "Wait for the great surprise on January 1." Public curiosity is piqued. There is much banter about the mysterious advertisements on the radio. The public impatiently waits for the great surprise to be revealed. But on December 31, the day before the great surprise, a cigarette manufacturer covers all of the billboards he can find with posters saying, "The great surprise is the new cigarette. . . ." Can the automobile manufacturer bring the cigarette manufacturer before a judge? What protection will he claim? Did the automobile manufacturer acquire a property right on the advertising? What would this right be based upon? Is this case different from the case regarding the fox? How?

Sutherland (1957) went on to say that, having shared this imaginary case in the classroom, it is hoped that a certain number of students would begin to speak, perhaps expressing opinions different from that of the first student questioned about the fox. If all goes well, the professor can now preside over an enthusiastic but orderly debate. The classroom of law students would be alive with the legal conversation. The other students who do not enter the debate would take careful notes, exactly as young people in other times learned the law by taking notes during court hearings.

Sutherland (1957) admitted that the process is time-consuming. His aim was to group cases and hypotheticals in such a way that the different facets of a legal principle were revealed and ambiguities explored, analyzed, and evaluated. Through this process, the students also could detect the development of the law. The first case about the fox brought to light a principle, and the second case regarding the billboard challenged students to apply this principle in an unforeseen manner. The sequence of hypotheticals guided the students to perceive the principle that informed the judge's ruling. The sequence of cases guided the students to apply the principle in an unexpectedly relevant contemporary context.

Socratic Elements of the Legal Adaptation

What makes the legal adaptation distinctively Socratic?

First, it is the inductive manner of selecting cases, problems, and hypotheticals to stimulate and extend analysis and judgment. A sequence of cases, real or fictional, presents a complex problem or principle from different points of view. A student must actively reason through the problems and be prepared to justify his or her interpretation. In the same way that Socrates selected different concepts as problems, and then analyzed alternative points of view, so a student examines different possible interpretations of the law and seeks to establish which is most justified. Students cannot rely on rote memory or the simple application of a rule.

Second, to complicate and extend the exploration further, short hypotheticals, ideally "one line long, often focusing on a single, easily stated fact" (Areeda, 1996), may be used to explore a continuum of possible interpretations in a creative and memorable manner (Gewirtz, 1982). Like Socrates, the instructor asks questions rather than lecturing answers. The thinking is done by the students. The aim is to ignite informed analytical debate in the students. The sequence of Socratic questions will likely include recitation questions oriented to memory, regarding terms, facts, and opinions, but there will be far more analysis and judgment questions present than memory questions.

The ratio of student talk to professor talk favors the students. Sutherland (1957) wryly mentioned that "it is hoped" that students begin to share and debate opinions (p. 558). A number of variables, as teachers know, impact student participation in discussion. Principally, the climate of the classroom (and of the school as a whole), the expectations and skills of the teacher, and the preparation and disposition of the students can foster or inhibit the discussion.

The Art of the Hypothetical

Thought experiments have a long history in philosophy (Brown & Fehige, 2014; Solum, 2015). Dennett (2013) called them intuition pumps because of the insights they can generate. Legal hypotheticals are small thought experiments that can be creatively used in myriad ways to stimulate analysis and judgment.

First, hypotheticals may be used to articulate the complexity of an important term or concept. Areeda (1996) demonstrated this in an example from contract law that used the term *offer*. A judge ruled that a document in a case was not an offer because the word *offer* was not explicitly used. Areeda then asked students a hypothetical: Is a contract made when Smith says, "I offer to sell my new $500 skies for one dollar" and Jones says, "I accept"? The exchange, Areeda wittily added, was witnessed by 20 skiing bishops, and Smith had just fallen many times while skiing. In response to this hypothetical, students offered their opinions and their reasoning—in the same way students might respond to Langdell's (1873) questions on his examinations (see Chapter 3). By using more hypotheticals and generating more discussion, a consensus then emerged. Although Areeda did not use the phrase *necessary and sufficient conditions*, by using hypothetical examples and counterexamples, he wished for students to focus the necessary and sufficient conditions for a legal offer. Once students understood the complexity of the term *offer*—and it was clear that the mere use of the word was insufficient—this understanding was applied to support or contest the ruling in the original case. Rather than accept the utterance of an authority, the students were guided to quasi-reflective thinking (King & Kitchener 1994, 2002).

Next, hypotheticals can be used to test the applicability of rules or principles. Changing the hypothetical pattern of facts demonstrates how the application of a principle or rule can change (Katz & O'Neill, 2009). In one set of circumstances, the application is clear and justified, but with each new alteration of facts focusing on one element, the applicability slips slightly. The sequence leads from a black-and-white reality to a gray scale of possibility. Making students aware of the gray scale of legal interpretation is one of the chief purposes of hypotheticals.

The term *fact pattern* is especially useful for visualizing and understanding the possibilities of hypotheticals. The facts in the legal problem present a pattern that must be interpreted; if an aspect of the pattern changes significantly (a fact alters), then the interpretation of the situation may change significantly as well. Rissland (1983) observed that hypotheticals may change the action itself, the sequence of events, the place of the event, the context of the action, or the attributes of the defendant or plaintiff (see Figure 5). Sometimes the order of hypotheticals is important, and at other times it is not. What is important is to clearly understand what aspect of the law will be highlighted through the sequence.

Imaginative and playful hypotheticals may agreeably color a questioning style. As discussed previously, Sutherland (1957) used an imaginative hypothetical of a fox shown in country fairs abandoning theatrical life. This humor can become a leitmotif of Socratic questioning. At first unexpected and perplexing, the humor underlines a principle and may also make a principle more memorable.

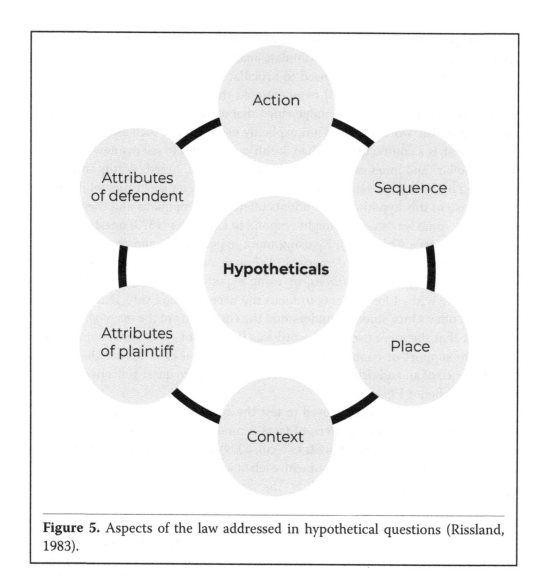

Figure 5. Aspects of the law addressed in hypothetical questions (Rissland, 1983).

Outside of the classroom, an illustration of the versatility of hypotheticals for stimulating astute and subtle analysis and judgment can be seen in the Supreme Court's oral arguments in *Masterpiece Cakeshop v. Colorado Civil Rights Commission*. Justice Elena Kagan identified three axes for exploration in the examination of the issues of freedom of speech and freedom of religion when in tension with public accommodation and antidiscrimination laws. The first axis is what constitutes speech and nonspeech (i.e., Is the creation of a wedding cake a speech act, and, if so, should it be protected by the First Amendment?). The second axis is whether the case only concerns gay people, or whether it raises the same issue with regard to race, gender, religion, etc. The third axis is whether the issue solely concerns weddings, or whether other ceremonies are also implicated (e.g., Bar Mitvahs, First

Communions, anniversaries, birthdays, etc.). A fourth axis that later surfaced is the status of the corporation and the employee. Can an employee refuse a service on the basis of personal religious belief? Each axis was explored through hypotheticals.

Another hypothetical sequence, notorious and often-dreaded, is the slippery slope (Lode, 1999). There are two ways to understand the slippery slope—in informal logic and in legal teaching. In informal logic, a slippery slope is a logical fallacy that seeks a series of agreements that lead inexorably to a negative outcome. For example, one might oppose measures of gun control with the belief that any regulation will lead to a ban on gun ownership. The first step of regulation, it is held, leads inexorably to the final step of banning gun ownership. In legal teaching, the slippery slope is a series of hypotheticals that lead to an unforeseen and unexpected outcome; it is not a logical fallacy. Areeda (1996) pointed out that hypotheticals are commonly misused to spring traps on students. For example, a professor might ask how a student stands on an issue and then ask why the student takes this stand. No matter how the student answers, the professor then formulates a series of hypotheticals that pushes the student down a chute of affirmations and, in the end, reveals a serious flaw in judgment. In this case, the student feels like a means for the professor's demonstration of superior judgment. To prevent such an impression, Areeda suggested disclosing the two ends of the slippery slope—that is, the apparently innocuous beginning and the clearly undesirable ending—so that the examination of the intermediary area is possible without anyone feeling humiliated.

SUMMARY
Hypotheticals

Change the agent, the attributes of the agent, the action, the context, or the sequence of events:

▸ to draw out the complexity of a concept,

▸ to test a rule or principle (what are its consequences in another situation?),

▸ to inject humor or drama that will make a principle or rule more memorable, or

▸ to demonstrate an unforeseen outcome through a series of hypotheticals (a slippery slope).

ONE METHOD, MANY STYLES

From the earliest years, there were significant differences in how professors practiced the legal adaptation of the Socratic Method (Gray, 1888). Scott Turow's (1977) classic memoir of his experience at Harvard Law makes this clear as well. Professors approached the legal adaptation with different tones. Some dwelled on one case at length, and others considered many. Some professors never made a positive statement and taught entirely through questioning. Some professors cold-called, randomly selecting students for questioning. Some were acerbic, and some were kind. Nonetheless, even considering the variety of personal interpretations and the differing degrees of mastery, the legal adaptation appears to be the most rigorous adaptation of Socratic Method. It is the closest to what one sees within the dialogues by Plato and Xenophon. Arguably, it improves on it.

Like the Renaissance variation from which it descends, this method begins with the selection of an ill-structured problem or a series of ill-structured problems. The teacher is conscious of the issues linking the sequence. What is important is not the simple application of a rule to a case, but the careful analysis and evaluation of the complex structure of the facts and how they relate to the complex body of law. There is a need for subtle interpretation, with teachers keeping in mind consequences and implications. Altering the facts in the problem (or pattern) alters the interpretation. Through reasoning with hypotheticals, students extend their knowledge.

Unlike an authoritarian exchange between professor and pupil, this method can empower a democratic and engaged group discussion and debate. Without unraveling into laissez-faire anarchy, the discussion remains informed and analytical. One measure of the legal variation's efficacy is whether the students can leap into discussion with their own arguments, ideas, and hypotheticals (Lepaulle, 1920; Sutherland, 1957). Everyone becomes Socrates. The maieutic portion of the conversation would at least require the preparation of short hypotheticals to test the key principles in unexpected ways. As Chief Justice Roberts observed, by sowing doubt, one reaps insight.

This variation also can be adapted very easily to secondary school education. There are excellent programs for teaching law in high school (see https://www. streetlaw.org). Teachers can prepare a class simulation of an oral argument before the Supreme Court. But the legal variation can also be transposed to the teaching of ethics, a subject found within many other subject areas (e.g., literature, art, history, science, current events), in which moral judgments are made or discussed. The problems are moral dilemmas, found within the local or international news or within imaginary scenarios. One must arrive at the discussion of principles to sort and justify positions. Perhaps one must face the prioritizing of values or rights.

For a sample lesson plan using the legal variation, see the Appendix. This sample lesson asks, "What is art?"—a vexing question that permits a variety of answers and calls attention to how knowledge is constructed by communities.

THE LEGAL VARIATION
Steps

1. Select a problem or a series of problems.
2. Draft the content and exploratory questions. Begin with the facts.
3. Prepare sequences of hypotheticals for exploring the axes and continua of the principles or concepts.
4. Prepare a choice of extension activities.

CHAPTER 5

SOCRATIC ROLE-PLAYING

Tell me, I forget,
Teach me and I may remember,
Involve me and I learn.

—Benjamin Franklin

ROLE-PLAYING IN THE CLASSROOM

Using the Socratic Method within role-playing is probably the most entertaining adaptation for students and teacher alike. Popular games, such as *Dungeons and Dragons*, as well as many contemporary online games, have made role-playing familiar to students. Role-playing in the classroom should be distinguished from sociodrama and psychodrama, which are used in therapy and counselling (Blatner, 2000; Sternberg & Garcia 2000). It can also be distinguished from simulations. Role-playing requires assuming an identity for the purposes of discussion or debate; simulations require assuming a role as well as imitating the processes and procedures of an organization or event. For instance, having students assume the identities of world leaders for the purpose of discussion is role-playing; having the stu-

DOI: 10.4324/9781003238089-6

dents assume the identities of world leaders as well as carry out the procedures for a crisis meeting of the Security Council of the United Nations is a simulation.

Both activities create an emotionally intense, spontaneous, and multifaceted experience for memorable learning. Simulations often require more extensive preparation. In the popular Model United Nations conferences, which began at Syracuse University as the Model League of Nations and were recast after the founding of the UN following World War II, students become delegates from the world's nations and consultative nongovernmental organizations. After weeks of preparation requiring research into the nations and organizations as well as into complex and urgent contemporary issues and policies, the student delegates gather to discuss and debate possible practical solutions to the issues. Through the simulation, they develop important and transferable skills in research, writing, collaboration, communication, and debate. They take on responsibilities, and they have tremendous fun. But preparation takes time.

Non-Socratic role-playing may be found in different classes. Language classes commonly use role-playing to develop skills in expression; participants can assume the identities of characters in plays, stories, and novels, and in this manner, enter more deeply into the complexities of the works. In history and political science classes, role-playing has been used to study the American Revolution, the English Civil War, and other crises (Gorvine, 1970). In science classes, it has been used to study mitosis and muscle contraction (Hudson, 2003; Stamper, 1973; Wyn & Stegink, 2000). Role-playing has also been used to teach students about significant moments in the history of science (Randak, 1990). Teachers may impersonate historical figures for their classes to render the content more approachable and memorable. For example, a teacher might impersonate Charles Darwin, Galileo, or Gregor Mendel in a science class. Moments from the history of mathematics or applications of mathematics concepts can also be used (Johnston-Wilder, Lee, & Pimm, 2017). Role-playing has been used in law-related education as well as in values education (Gallagher, 1979).

Socratic role-playing can be organized more quickly than a simulation. It permits the students to consider and understand alternative points of view, scaffolding the passage from prereflective thinking and its reliance on absolutist and authoritarian reasoning (King & Kitchener, 1994, 2002). Role-playing creates a kind of virtual reality for understanding other points of view. By delving into how other people regard a particular issue or problem, students reconsider and perhaps modify their own positions. From the very beginning of the activity, role-playing in the classroom encourages students to explore comparisons and contrasts.

Through maieutic questioning, a Socratic moderator may then lead the discussion into unforeseen areas of a case, in which the participants, rather than simply restate well-known concepts or ideas, must actively react to a fluid situation and examine the assumptions, consequences, and implications of these ideas and concepts. Students must move from quick and reflexive System 1 thinking to engage in more effortful and reflective System 2 thinking (Kahneman, 2011). Through this experience, guided purposefully into the gray areas of issues and dilemmas, the participants memorably learn how to orient themselves and refine their judgment.

A role-playing discussion can be framed in different ways. As Thompson (1978) observed, it may be based on an experience from the past, the present, or the future. It may be fantasy or reality, a personal issue or a societal problem. It may reflect concepts or a controversy. One way to set up a discussion is to select a group of figures to speak about a question, issue, or problem, with each expressing a point of view. Another way is to propose an issue suggested within an evolving story; each participant must not simply express a point of view, but react to a changing narrative that challenges easy reactions.

THE SOCRATIC MODERATOR

As with the other adaptations, we may ask "how" and "to what extent" does the moderation of a role-playing discussion become distinctively Socratic. Socrates did not moderate discussions for others. He did not coordinate the contributions of a group of individuals—probing, challenging, complicating, and summarizing. He did not underline the comparisons and contrasts. He did not assume a role in a story.

But there are nonetheless several Socratic characteristics in this activity that foster logical reasoning and informed, balanced judgment. There is an open, ill-structured problem focused on a network of urgent issues about which reasonable people may disagree. These issues require analysis and evaluation of concepts and reasoning. During the discussion, the moderator (teacher) can solicit diverse points of view and the reasoning and evidence supporting them. The complications in the story inductively challenge participants to engage in thoughtful, reflective analysis and evaluation of the issues.

Next, in conducting the discussion, the moderator does not represent a point of view and refrains from making positive statements and judgments. She does, however, exhibit Socratic curiosity and ignorance. She must principally ask open questions, guiding the discussion forward. The questions may also reflectively summarize or seek clarification and evidence. The moderator seeks to uncover and test interpretations, assumptions, consequences, and implications. She may offer a hypothetical. She seeks to bring different points of view to bear on an issue or situation. The participants should not be interacting repeatedly with the moderator; they should be speaking with each other. At times, the moderator can set up these interactions explicitly (e.g., asking that Charles Darwin explain his theory to William Jennings Bryan, and then asking Bryan to respond). The Socratic moderator should not dominate the discussion, and the ratio of talk should clearly favor the participants. In these ways, the moderator Socratically facilitates the interaction of the participants.

The clever advice given by Jean Le Clerc (1700) more than 300 years ago is helpful for Socratic moderation: The moderator must want to learn from the participants, must ask for clarification of any difficult words or terms, must probe with curiosity the details of answers, and must seek examples and comparisons.

Depending on the type of discussion, the maieutic questions might include:

- What options do you have?
- What would you do?
- Why would you do that?
- What is your reasoning?
- What do you mean by . . . ?
- Can you clarify . . . ?
- How would you react to what _____ said?
- What if _____ were to happen?

Joan Greco (2010a, 2010b, 2010c, 2010d, 2010e, 2010f, 2011, 2017), a savvy organizer of Socratic role-playing discussions who worked extensively on the Fred Friendly Seminars (see the following section), gave excellent advice for moderating. In a gently skeptical spirit similar to Le Clerc's (1700), Greco (2010e) suggested telling students, "Walk me through it. Take us step by step and show us how it happens" (para. 3).

One especially insightful piece of advice regards phrasing questions in the negative. Given the general propensity of people to disagree with others and to push back against moderators, Greco (2010f) recommended phrasing questions in the negative. By doing so, the teacher innocently takes the other side in formulating a question in order for the respondent to contradict the suggestion and expand upon the reasoning for the contradiction (e.g., "Science is about hard and measurable facts, isn't it? There is nothing theoretical about it, right?").

EXAMPLE SOCRATIC ROLE-PLAYING DIALOGUES

One can see striking and expert demonstrations of the Socratic Method in its role-playing variation in the Fred Friendly Seminars, which have been televised in the United States since the 1980s (Engelman, 2009). A former president of CBS, Fred Friendly began the seminars in 1974, following Watergate, with an experimental seminar attended by 50 lawyers, judges, and journalists and moderated by law professors Arthur R. Miller, Charles Nesson, and Abraham S. Goldstein. Friendly's aim was to bring journalists and judges together to talk about difficult issues and, in this manner, diffuse the post-Watergate tensions between journalism and the law. Aired on PBS, this series assembled experts from different fields for exploration of thorny civil, political, legal, and ethical issues. The discussions were moderated chiefly by distinguished law professors who were skilled in Socratic teaching and who moderated with agility and wit. One observer accurately called the moderators "politely aggressive" (Medicine and the Media, 1980). Selected series have excellent teaching guides.

A reporter (Jones, 1987) recounted the genesis of a typical episode. First, the staff composed a hypothetical scenario (in this instance, a terrorist hijacking), and this scenario was tested on an untelevised seminar led by Friendly. Using this experience, the staff further refined the hypothetical situation and the questions for the moderator. With this more refined scenario, Friendly would begin to invite appropriate qualified experts to participate in the televised seminar. A month before the taping, he would do another dry run with other experts (not those in the televised version) in a conference room at Columbia University. With the moderator watching, the experts offered advice to sharpen the questions further. On the eve of the seminar, the moderator and the staff further polished the scenario and the questions.

Friendly said that he sought to achieve the "agony quotient" eight or nine times during the seminar (as cited in Jones, 1987, para. 13). By this he meant that a significant question should force a participant into unexpected and challenging thinking, not an automatic response. When the actual seminar began, the invited participants had only a general idea of the topic, and the moderator had an outline; thus, the preparation had been careful, but the responses would be spontaneous. Each 3-hour discussion was edited for a 1-hour broadcast (Meyerson, 1985).

What was the process of the role-playing Socratic dialogue in this case? The moderator would recount a fictional story often based on recent news stories. There was always a problem, a crisis, or a dilemma. In some seminars, the moderator might assume the role of the protagonist in the story. The participants were then invited to assume roles within the story. Usually an expert assumed the role of his particular expertise (e.g., a judge, a member of a political party, a cabinet member, etc.), thus bringing a wealth of knowledge, insight, and experience to the discussion. The story would proceed to a crisis point. The moderator then would ask one of the participants to react to the story and explain the reasoning for the reaction (i.e., "What would you do, and why would you do this?"). Then, opposing or alternative points of view were sought.

For example, in a scenario moderated by Miller (1982), Artie, who was middle-aged and has lost many relatives to colon cancer, was pondering whether he should seek genetic screening to determine whether he possessed the gene that would likely cause him to become ill in the same manner. Participants assume the roles of his sister, his physician, and a genetic counselor. The discussion explored three larger themes (each 12–15 minutes in length): that the results of genetic tests can have unintended consequences, that the ownership and security of genetic information is unclear, and that many may seek the genetic information for conflicting purposes. A steady flow of questions carried the Socratic simulation forward:

- ▶ How would the results affect your mental well-being?
- ▶ What if your employer or insurer discovered the results? Does either have a right to know?
- ▶ If a person is adopting a child, should the child be tested for this gene?
- ▶ Should candidates for important government positions be screened for this gene?

Many other questions explored the issue in an enlightening manner.

PREPARATION FOR CLASS ROLE-PLAYING

The preparation for role-playing varies according to the instructional goals and how much time a teacher wishes to dedicate to the discussion in class. Obviously, a short discussion among three students is easier to organize than a more extended discussion among nine or more. This activity can be done to present content in a dramatic way, or it can be done to review content dramatically. A more articulated understanding of concepts or situations does require more time because students must feel comfortable with the ideas in order to think actively, not merely read from a script. The phases of preparation are as follows, and each will be discussed in detail.

PHASES OF SOCRATIC ROLE-PLAYING

1. Select an issue according to the class objectives.
2. Write the Socratic scenario(s) and question outline.
3. Assign the roles and schedule conferences.

4. Discussion: thinking aloud/thinking allowed.

5. Prepare a choice of extension activities.

STEP 1: SELECT AN ISSUE ACCORDING TO THE CLASS OBJECTIVES

Issues for Socratic discussion are embedded within curricula according to specific objectives and standards. Controversial issues are most helpful, and teachers can layer issues within a problem or real-life situation. For example, climate changes is addressed in the NGSS in elementary, middle, and high school. The issue of climate change invites examination from the viewpoints of science, business, ethics, politics, and the law. How have scientists reached a consensus about the change in climate? How should businesses react to the challenges of climate change? Is it ethical to lobby to block policies that combat climate change? How would one incentivize net-zero emissions by 2050? How would such a law be enforced?

Controversial issues are omnipresent in the news. Teachers can survey the issues on which the United Nations works. There are also websites such as iSide-With (https://www.isidewith.com) whose polls indicate positions on issues as well as elections. The issues used in the classroom must be open questions that permit extended reflective reasoning; in this way, there is justifiably more than one reasonable point of view for students to investigate.

Teach Like Socrates (Wilberding, 2014) suggests philosophical concepts and provides advice on how to research them. The works of Stephen Law (2003), Julian Baggini (2003; Baggini & Fosl, 2010; Baggini & Kraus, 2012), and Nigel Warburton (2008, 2013) are also lucid and helpful in providing accurate and accessible summaries of philosophical positions.

As an example, let us consider the topic of animal rights. First, we must define what we mean by this term: What do we mean by an *animal*? What do we mean by a *right*? Are all animals in the same category? Do we expect some animals to have rights identical to human rights? What is a moral community? What aspect of animal rights can we examine in class (e.g., cosmetic testing, clothing, sports, zoos, meat consumption, scientific experimentation, cloning)?

Then, we must understand the basic concepts and the ramifications of the issue—how it branches out and touches other concepts and issues. Concept mapping (Novak & Gowin, 1984) is one manner of understanding this topography, allowing learners to see the boundaries of ideas and how overlapping occurs. This also permits students and teachers to simplify or complicate more consciously the facts within the problem. Students cannot investigate, analyze, and evaluate all of the issues regarding animal rights within a single class. But they can combine a limited number of issues and provide insights into the complex nature of the matter.

If we select the animal rights topic, we can then formulate an issue: *To what extent, if at all, is it ethically permissible to clone animals for the medical benefit of human beings?* The concepts that need precise definition through research include:

- animal;
- rights;
- ethics;
- the principals of reduction, refinement, and replacement;
- experiment;
- cloning; and
- speciesism.

STEP 2: WRITE THE SOCRATIC SCENARIO(S) AND QUESTION OUTLINE

With an issue in mind, a teacher can then imagine a difficult or interesting scenario for that issue. Hypothetical scenarios give greater freedom for discussion. As in fiction, crisis and conflict create interest. Dilemmas force students to make decisions that will be guided by one principle but will somehow compromise another. By writing a more generalized problem based on current events, removing specific identities and places, the teacher raises the discussion to a level of abstraction that permits the examination of principles, concepts, and values. The scenario develops complications so that alternative points of view emerge. It can be helpful to understand the scenario as a fact pattern, as in the legal variation. The teacher first establishes discrete facts or details that will be modified in the developing scenario(s). Using such details to paint a picture makes the scenario more memorable (Greco, 2010d).

Representative figures in the scenario can also help students explore alternative points of view. Issues that have a personal dimension (i.e., that affect students' family and/or friends) are more accessible. Teachers can unite persons from diverse eras (e.g., Machiavelli can debate with John Locke) or have students role-play in a fictional country or local context (e.g., students might role-play the issue of illegal Roma camps in the city). Teachers can also make the role-play interdisciplinary, demonstrating the interconnectedness of knowledge, by selecting figures from diverse disciplines. With regard to the animal cloning issue discussed previously, students' roles might include a scientist in favor of animal cloning, a scientist who opposes cloning, and an ethicist who reviews the possible criteria for judgment.

For the lesson, cloning arguably becomes more controversial as one moves from the vegetable to the animal kingdom. When I have presented this issue in the classroom, I have tried to use the contexts of family and friends to make the issues more personal and accessible. Teachers can present the problems concerning cloning by beginning with plants and moving by steps to animals, presenting different motivations for cloning: culinary, educational, personal, and scientific. This approach can easily be modified to help students examine the issues surrounding Genetically Modified Organisms (GMOs).

Socratic Scenarios. The following six scenarios present the issue of cloning in different contexts. The sequence begins with vegetables and then proceeds through animals.

▶ **Vegetables.** Let's say it is a Sunday in early April. You are driving through the countryside with your family and you want some organic fruit and vegetables. You stop at a stand near the road, where a farmer and his 8-year-old son are selling fresh produce. The little boy tells you that the potatoes are part of his science project for school because they are clones. "What?" you ask. "Clones?" He explains that his potatoes may naturally reproduce through cloning. When he cuts the potato up and plants the pieces, each potato that grows is a natural clone. Would you buy the cloned potatoes? Why or why not?

▶ **Animals for Food.** You offer to take your family out to eat for lunch, and they vote on sushi. So, you take your family to a sushi restaurant, where they begin considering whether to order the bluefin tuna. Today some of the most expensive sushi in the world is made from bluefin tuna, which holds the record as the most expensive food of all time. In early 2019, a restaurant owner in Japan paid $3.1 million for a 612-pound bluefin tuna (Repanich, 2019). But suppose that a few years ago scientists succeeded in cloning the fish and farming it, causing it to cost just twice as much as regular fresh tuna—expensive, but affordable on a special occasion. This particular restaurant offers the cloned tuna. Would you order the cloned bluefin tuna sushi for your family? Are you curious? Why or why not?

▶ **Animals for a Zoo.** After lunch, you decide to take your family to the zoo. But this zoo is special, for it has some of the rarest animals on the planet. There is the Amur leopard, the northern sportive lemur, and the saola, a gentle bovid discovered in 1992 and found only in Vietnam and Laos. This zoo has clones of the saola. Would you take your family to see clones of this endangered species? Why or why not?

▶ **Animals for Pets.** Your dog, a Chow Chow, is your constant companion—affectionate and loyal. He seems to understand exactly what you think and feel. When you come home at the end of the day, before you open the front door, you can hear him jumping and barking with excitement. If you take a trip, he falls into melancholy and mopes under your favorite chair. There is a powerful bond between you. Now, after years of friendship, you realize your Chow Chow is aging. You can have him cloned—it costs a lot of money, but you can do it. Would you clone your pet? Why or why not? Are there any life lessons in confronting the reality of aging?

▶ **Animals for Drugs.** You are a venture capitalist who needs to decide where to invest a large sum of money. A pharmaceutical company has a new process for producing a drug to treat dengue fever, an infectious disease carried by mosquitoes. Forty percent of the world's population is at risk of catching this disease. The new process consists of altering the genes of cows, which then create the antiviral drug in their blood. Suppose that cloning the transgenic cows will produce the drug at a fraction of the cost for the market, making a cure more available for the world. It would also be a very lucrative investment; you would make a lot of money. Would you invest in this pharmaceutical company? Why or why not?

▶ **Animals for Research.** There are some terrible diseases that affect humans. Many of us know people who have been tragically afflicted by Alzheimer's and Parkinson's. We already clone plants and livestock for food. We can also clone animals to understand and combat diseases that devastate the population. Genetic disorders can be better understood with the cloning of animals. But doing so also requires afflicting these animals with the diseases and manipulating their genes to better understand what causes the affliction. Would you permit the cloning of macaque monkeys, as has been done in China, to improve human understanding of these diseases? Why or why not?

Question Outline. Creating a question outline is important for maintaining students' focus during discussion. In broad terms, the questions fall into three categories: *basic questions* to review content, *exploratory questions* to reveal the personal understanding of the students, and *analytical questions* to examine this understanding more closely (Wilberding, 2014). In the discussion, there is a rhythm of basic, exploratory, and analytical questions. The rhythm is not a simple sequence, but may be adapted according to the judgment of the teacher. For instance, teachers need not ask all of the content questions at once. They can also repeat questions at intervals to different students. Teachers might consider which questions are appropriate for which students.

For the cloning discussion, the basic, exploratory, and analytical questions include the following.

▶ Basic Questions:
  ▷ What is *cloning*?
  ▷ How is cloning done in the laboratory?

    ▷ What is a *right*?
    ▷ What is "equal consideration of interest"?
    ▷ What are different motivations for cloning?
    ▷ What does *transgenic* mean?
    ▷ Who was Jeremy Bentham?
    ▷ What is *speciesism*?

▶ Exploratory Questions:
    ▷ Is it important to define what an animal is to understand this issue? Don't we all know what an animal is?
    ▷ Do animals have rights?
    ▷ How can we reconcile disagreements about whether animals have rights?
    ▷ What is the difference between a philosophical belief and a religious belief?
    ▷ Are zoos ethical? Is it ethical to have a pet?
    ▷ What are the advantages of animal experimentation?
    ▷ What are the disadvantages of animal experimentation?
    ▷ Is animal experimentation an occasion of speciesism on the part of human beings?
    ▷ Should animals be genetically altered for human beings to make money?
    ▷ What are some of the religious positions on the issue of cloning?
    ▷ Should science be limited by ethics?
    ▷ Should scientific research be granted complete freedom to improve our knowledge and our lives?

▶ Analytical Questions:
    ▷ How can we argue that animals have rights?
    ▷ How can we argue that animals do not have rights?
    ▷ How can we prioritize human lives above the lives of animals?

STEP 3: ASSIGN THE ROLES AND SCHEDULE CONFERENCES

The Socratic role-playing discussion includes the entire class. Teachers should inform the students about the format of the discussion and what the expectations for participation are. Students should be reminded to listen actively, speak respectfully and kindly, and regard civil disagreement as a welcome opportunity to help clarify ideas.

By assigning the same roles to several students, a teacher can prepare all of the students in the class. Alternatively, a teacher can assign a restricted number of students with individual expert roles but then include the entire class in discussion. Meaningful role-playing requires much preparation from the students; they must be knowledgeable about the issues and aware of their individual roles. Often this preparation determines students' levels of participation. If students do not prepare, they will feel inhibited and unsure of themselves during discussion or may remain silent. See Figure 6 for websites, articles, and other resources that can help students as they research their roles.

The following roles are used within the animal cloning role-play:

▸ **A scientist in favor of animal cloning.** This student will be prepared to explain the basic science of cloning. Her point of view is that the cloning of animals will permit the advancement of the study of genetic disease, including cancer and metabolic and immune disorders (Briggs, 2018). She should discuss how cloning follows the ethical standards of the U.S. National Institutes of Health.

▸ **A scientist in opposition to animal cloning.** This student will also be prepared to explain the basic science of cloning. However, he will take a negative approach by citing some of the drawbacks: that the vast majority of cloning attempts end in failure, that clones develop genetic diseases and suffer terribly, and that the cost in pain is enormous.

▸ **An ethicist.** This student will understand and be able to explain the following questions: What is a right? What are animal rights? How might one argue that animals have or do not have rights?

▸ **A venture capitalist.** This student feels that her primary duty is to shareholders and would like to make money in her investments. She should be able to discuss the following: Should business be influenced by concerns about ethics?

▸ **An animal welfare activist.** This student takes the side of the animals on all occasions. He should be familiar with arguments supporting animal rights.

▸ **A religious authority.** This student may represent any religion but must have a coherent and principle-based position on the issue.

STEP 4: THE DISCUSSION: THINKING ALOUD/THINKING ALLOWED

A Socratic moderator must be focused entirely on fostering polite and engaged student participation. Each classroom has its own climate, depending on the teacher and the students, as well as on the climate in other classes and the school

Genetics and Cloning

▶ Learn.Genetics: Cloning (https://learn.genetics.utah.edu/content/cloning): Composed by the Genetics Science Learning Center of the University of Utah and approved by the National Science Teachers Association, this site reviews the basic science of cloning, its history, its purpose, and the myths surrounding it.

Animal Ethics

▶ BBC Ethics Guide: Animal Ethics (https://www.bbc.co.uk/ethics/animals): This site provides an overview of different positions on animal ethics and includes religious positions. Legal facts are contextualized to the United Kingdom.

▶ "Rights" by Manuel Velasquez, Claire Andrew, Thomas Shanks, S.J., and Michael J. Meyer (https://www.scu.edu/ethics/ethics-resources/ethical-decision-making/rights): This text incisively reviews the question "What is a right?", negative and positive rights, and conflicts of rights. It does not cover animal rights.

▶ *Animal Rights: A Very Short Introduction* by David DeGrazia: Part of the extraordinary series of succinct introductions on a vast spectrum of topics, this book examines the moral status of animals; the harms of suffering, confinement, and death; the issues of meat eating, pets, and zoos; and animal research.

▶ "Non-Human Animals: Crash Course Philosophy #42" by CrashCourse (https://www.youtube.com/watch?v=y3-BX-jN_Ac): This video, presented by Hank Green, gives a 10-minute overview of the moral considerations regarding animals, the views of Peter Singer and Carl Cohen, and the concept of equal consideration of interest.

Animal Experimentation and Cloning

▶ "It's Time to Question Bio-engineering" by Paul Root Wolpe (https://www.ted.com/talks/paul_root_wolpe_it_s_time_to_question_bio_engineering): This TED Talk puts bioengineering into perspective. A large part of the video reviews the astonishing achievements of bioengineering in the last 20 years.

▶ Speaking of Research (https://speakingofresearch.com): This organization, founded in 2008, seeks to inform readers on the necessity and benefits of animal experimentation for medical progress.

▶ End Animal Cloning (http://www.endanimalcloning.org): This activist website seeks to inform the public about animal cloning.

Figure 6. Resources for the animal cloning role-play.

as a whole. Students quickly understand which teachers genuinely permit personal or alternative points of view to be expressed. Authoritarian teachers who bluntly quash incorrect answers may always be right, but they have not allowed the class to Socratically and cooperatively explore, analyze, and evaluate a position, leaving students entrenched and unchallenged in the prereflective stage of development (King

& Kitchener, 1994, 2002). In other words, the students may know "the answer," but they have not necessarily understood its justification or cause. A more democratic atmosphere in the classroom fosters more spontaneous participation.

Every discussion group is different. The moderator must bring out the basic facts and explore the issues with the entire class, making judicious and continuous use of the student experts. This does not mean running through the outline of basic questions in a linear manner, asking everyone the same question. A moderator should begin with the scenario and then seek the personal responses of students and the student experts in their roles, drawing out content to help students more explicitly inform their positions. In this way, a moderator can discover the dialectic within the students.

At the end of the discussion, in the last 10 minutes of class, the moderator returns to the question: *To what extent, if at all, is it ethically permissible to clone animals for the medical benefit of human beings?* What are the students' views now?

ROLES OF THE SOCRATIC MODERATOR

The Socratic moderator:

▸ begins and continues the scenario(s) to advance discussion;

▸ asks questions to seek clarification, add challenge, and help students consider consequences and connections;

▸ is curious and enthusiastic about all statements by participants (no sarcasm);

▸ makes no positive statements for one side or another of an issue (e.g., makes no indication or insinuation about the value of cloning);

▸ draws out basic content from the participants through open questioning;

▸ succinctly rephrases participants' remarks, *but does not add to them*;

▸ encourages interaction among the participants;

▸ encourages participants to question each other;

▸ discovers the dialectic within the participants;

▸ takes the other side (if necessary and only for a moment) to challenge agreement among participants; and

▸ may provocatively phrase selected questions in the negative (e.g., Doesn't cloning occur in nature?).

Typical questions include:

▸ What would you do?

▸ Why would you do that?

▸ What is your reasoning?

▸ What do you mean by . . . ?

▸ Can you clarify . . . ?

▸ How would you react to what _____ said?

▸ What if _____ were to happen?

▸ Let's assume that _____ . What would you think?

▸ Can you take us step by step through what you mean?

STEP 5: EXTENSION

What will the students take away from the discussion? The students should reflect on the different points of view and have a better understanding about animal rights, animal experimentation, and animal cloning. At the least, the students can write a reflection on the following question: *To what extent, if at all, is it ethically permissible to clone animals for the medical benefit of human beings?*

However, using the suggestion of Sternberg and Grigorenko (2004), teachers can also provide a choice of analytic, practical, and creative activities to extend thinking. The following are possible examples:

▸ Write an editorial arguing either side of the issue of animal cloning. (Analytical.)

▸ Write a philosophical dialogue on these questions: *Should ethics guide science? Whose ethics should guide it?* (Analytical.)

▸ Write an argumentative essay on this question: *If the law permits cloning, does this mean that cloning is ethical?* (Analytical.)

▸ Organize a student assembly about the issue of animal testing. (Practical.)

▸ Organize a student assembly about the issue of animal cloning for food: *Is cloned food used within the supermarkets and restaurants?* (Practical.)

▸ Write and perform a song about animal rights. (Creative.)

▸ Plan and shoot a short film (or music video) about animal rights. (Creative.)

CREATING UNIQUE ROLE-PLAYING SCENARIOS

The role-playing Socratic variation is the dramatization of the legal variation applied to a wider range of issues and adapted for group discussion. A portion of the class acts out the scenario, and all students spontaneously react to the scenario's changes. The turns within the story become the hypotheticals that extend the issue in different directions. Then, all students may react and reflect upon the decisions that are made. The challenging sequence of problems is itself Socratic. As in the Renaissance adaptation, the teacher seeks to discover the dialectic within the students.

A very simple version of this variation is the well-known tram problem by Foot (1967), which is sometimes used in demonstrations of the Socratic Method (CTLStanford, 2013, 2015). The student assumes the role of the tram driver in the dilemma. The tram car is out of control and can only turn onto one of two tracks. On one track, five workers labor; on the other track, there is a single worker. Which turn should the tram driver make? Although this thought experiment and its variations are insightful (it has been used by Harvard philosopher Michael Sandel [2009] as well), its applications are limited. A fuller dramatization of any dilemma, using multiple roles, brings out other aspects and nuances of a problem and permits greater student participation.

For teachers, there is great freedom and freshness in imagining and drafting unique scenarios rather than relying on well-known examples. Teachers can incorporate current events that take the content from the classroom to the real world. Such scenarios are more easily contextualized for students.

CHAPTER 6

WRITING PHILOSOPHICAL DIALOGUES IN THE CLASSROOM

Students, as they are increasingly posed with problems relating to themselves in the world and with the world, will feel increasingly challenged and obliged to respond to that challenge.

—Paulo Freire

WHY WRITE DIALOGUES?

In 1765, Voltaire published an entertaining philosophical dialogue that is often read in philosophy classes in French secondary schools. In the dialogue, a capon and a fattened hen meet in the yard, each lamenting its violent and painful treatment at the hands of men; in order for their flesh to become more tender to eat, the capon had been emasculated and the hen had undergone a hysterectomy. Through their conversation Voltaire deftly and poignantly impugned the intolerance of men to animals and to each other. The darkly humorous dialogue finishes with the capon recounting how men even burn other human beings merely for their opinions. The fable is a small masterpiece that condemns how human beings unthinkingly follow

87

DOI: 10.4324/9781003238089-7

traditions to commit atrocious acts against others. In a few pages Voltaire demonstrated the wide possibilities of the philosophical dialogue.

Philosophical dialogues were once a common medium for presenting and considering complex ideas. At their best, dialogues permit an imaginative, powerful, subtle, and memorable analysis of ideas, in which multiple characters present and defend their different points of view. By reading, studying, and writing such dialogues, students may learn how to analyze arguments to a greater extent. Dialogue offers the possibility for a creative and personal critique of ideas and attitudes. Moreover, it can be assimilated into other creative activities in class, like animations and short films.

Like playwriting or screenwriting, philosophical dialogue is a tricky form. It seems very simple to write a conversation or interview, but a dialogue that examines ideas is more difficult. Giving students a general orientation in the possibilities of the philosophical dialogue is helpful, for a dialogue's form is more compressed and carefully constructed than an impromptu conversation. When students (or adults) are asked to write a dialogue without any previous instruction about the expectations and possibilities of the form, their dialogues often demonstrate a limited understanding of what may be achieved. Teachers might view these attempts as (perhaps disheartening) revelations of student understanding of an educational conversation. Without preparation, students will not efficiently analyze and evaluate ideas. Some students will write an information-filled lecture punctuated by questions, with each question followed by a paragraph of response. This kind of dialogue expresses the banking model of education explained by Freire (1996), in which the authoritarian teacher makes deposits and the obedient and meek students are the depositories. Other students will write an interview with shorter paragraphs that are descriptive, not analytical or evaluative. Still others will depict two characters whose points of view should collide forcefully, but there is no development of analysis or evaluation, only two diametrically opposed expositions. At times, this last strategy may be the expression of relativism, the belief that each person's point of view must be respected and unexamined, not subjected to analysis and evaluation. Students may also spend too much of the text setting up the conversation rather than approach ideas from the beginning. Only a few students may present informed arguments from different perspectives.

Studying philosophical dialogues permits students to understand the possibilities of the form. Teachers might provide a short overview of the history of the philosophical dialogue, similar to the following section, to show the arc of its development. Teachers can also read representative excerpts of philosophical dialogues in class, discussing the ideas and highlighting their formal qualities. By framing the assignments carefully, teachers can guide the students to seize the opportunity to write creatively, reflectively and analytically.

A SHORT HISTORY OF THE PHILOSOPHICAL DIALOGUE

Socrates was famously suspicious of the written word. He did not leave behind any poetry, aphorisms, letters, treatises, or written dialogues. But his followers Plato and Xenophon did compose dialogues, and generations of ancient writers also saw value in writing them. Aristotle wrote dialogues, but these apparently have not survived. Dialogues held a place in literature different from poetry or plays. They were a creative and imaginative medium for the examination of ideas. Later, the Roman orator and statesman Cicero wrote dialogues on many subjects, including friendship, old age, and the nature of the gods. Nearly 200 years after Cicero, Lucian wrote satirical philosophical dialogues in Greek that had a great influence on history and remain entertaining and instructive today. These four classical models (Plato, Xenophon, Cicero, and Lucian) demonstrate how the selection of famous or infamous people from the past, the choice of location, and the adroit use of humor can meaningfully contribute to philosophical speculation regarding important issues. Plato and Xenophon, and in some places Lucian, demonstrate the inductive method of questioning used by Socrates. Of the four writers, Plato is the most excellent.

During the Middle Ages, philosophers composed philosophical dialogues, and most of these fall within the pattern of teacher-student. Saint Augustine of Hippo, for example, wrote dialogues on teaching as well as on music. More than 100 years later, while in prison in Pavia awaiting trial for alleged crimes against the Ostrogoth king Theodoric, Boethius wrote the poignant and accessible *Consolation of Philosophy* in which he and Lady Philosophy converse about the existence and nature of evil, happiness, and free will. Some passages are markedly Socratic in form.

In the Renaissance, writers such as Erasmus, Thomas More, and Giordano Bruno, among many others, composed dialogues on a variety of issues in religion, philosophy, politics, and science. When Galileo wished to present his reasoning and evidence for the Copernican theory to a larger audience, he wrote *Dialogue Concerning the Two Chief World Systems*, which led to his trial and condemnation by the Inquisition. Bernard le Bovier de Fontenelle composed the charming *Conversations on the Plurality of Worlds*, presenting these Copernican ideas less controversially.

In the 18th century, as the Enlightenment began, writers continued to use philosophical dialogues to examine ideas. George Berkeley and David Hume composed sophisticated philosophical dialogues. Berkeley's *Three Dialogues Between Hylas and Philonous*, which has many markedly Socratic passages, denies the existence of matter and proposes that only ideas exist. Hume's *Dialogues Concerning Natural Religion* cleverly presents his critique of arguments for the existence of God. The

French *philosophes*, such as Voltaire, Rousseau, and Diderot, also wrote many brilliant examples (Mortier, 2002).

As the search for knowledge became more centered at the university in the 19th century, fewer authors used dialogues as the vehicle for the exploration and criticism of ideas. However, there were still many notable examples. The German philosopher Arthur Schopenhauer wrote vigorous dialogues on death, immortality, and religion. Maurice Joly wrote *The Dialogue in Hell Between Machiavelli and Montesquieu*, which so provoked Napoleon III that Joly was imprisoned for more than a year. Oscar Wilde's *Decay of Lying* wittily explored the relationship of art and imagination to life and nature; he reached counterintuitive conclusions that challenged the accepted notions of his day.

In the 20th century, sophisticated philosophers, such as Iris Murdoch (1986) and Paul Feyerabend composed philosophical dialogues respectively on art and knowledge. John Perry (1978), an emeritus philosophy professor at Stanford University, investigated the issue of identity and immortality in a dialogue set within a hospital, in which a student and a college chaplain visit their philosophy professor friend who has been mortally injured in a motorcycle accident.

The continuity and creativity of the philosophical dialogue as a form are striking. By reading and discussing a few excerpts in class with the students, noting the creative possibilities, teachers can acquaint students with this long tradition and prepare them for writing better dialogues. Students can compose careful and effective maieutic passages as Plato and Xenophon did. They can use humor and satire as Lucian did. They can create personifications as Boethius did. They can define points of view with persons as Galileo did. They can write a dialogue in the form of a fable, as Voltaire did masterfully. They can use people from the past, the present, or future.

Simply providing students with an overview of the possibilities enriches practice immensely. Left alone, many students often write dialogues that are disappointingly narrow teacher-student interviews or dry recitations. Reviewing the history of form opens the possibilities.

THE WRITING PROCESS: OUTLINE

In learning to write essays, many students first learn the tightly constructed five-paragraph essay format, in which each sentence and paragraph has a purpose and place. Learning this form may seem at first restrictive, but it teaches a valuable lesson in structure that later can be modified to greater complexity and length. Similarly, the content and structure of philosophical dialogues improves if students carefully outline the argument(s) before writing. In order to create an outline, students must first clearly understand the issue, concepts, arguments, and counterarguments (see Figure 7 for an example planning page). In terms of length, I recommend that dialogues be 3–4 pages double-spaced. It is possible to assign two students to a dialogue, but writing in larger groups can be challenging and frustrating.

The following advice may be helpful for students as they create their outlines:

- ▸ Do not simplify or caricature the opposing point of view.
- ▸ Select characters for whom the issue or argument is important.
- ▸ Consider using the Galileo format, which includes two characters with defined positions and a third who must reason about the two sides.
- ▸ Select a significant location for the dialogue.
- ▸ Begin immediately with the issue to be explored; do not spend too much time in establishing the situation and setting.
- ▸ Conflict creates interest and often reveals the boundaries of ideas or previously unrecognized shared territory.
- ▸ Ask yourself: *Where will the disagreement(s) be?*
- ▸ Use fresh and personal examples taken from your own experience rather than trite and conventional ones that could occur to anyone.
- ▸ Hypotheticals test ideas and principles.
- ▸ Maieutic passages must be carefully constructed.
- ▸ Depending on the issue, there need not be a tidy and definitive conclusion.
- ▸ Remember: *You are the philosopher.*

DIALOGUE ASSIGNMENT: SENSORY PERCEPTION

The Theory of Knowledge (TOK) course of the International Baccalaureate program uses philosophical dialogue as an accessible form for expressing, analyzing, and evaluating different perspectives—a key skill for the class. Among its aims, the course seeks to teach students the roles of various ways of knowing (e.g., reason, emotion, and imagination) in creating knowledge. For instance, in studying sensory perception, students examine the reception of stimuli by the senses and the perception of the world by the brain to consider how this complex interaction may advance or frustrate the acquisition of knowledge. This work reflects an old philosophical question regarding appearance and reality: If our senses are limited and untrustworthy, how can we really know about the external world? Phenomena such as optical illusions, color blindness, blindsight, auditory or visual hallucinations

---

Philosophical Dialogue Planning Sheet

Class: _____ Date: _____

Issue phrased as a question:

Key terms and definitions:

Setting:

Characters and their arguments:

Maieutic passage:

Conclusion:

Figure 7. Philosophical dialogue planning sheet.

(such as Bonnet's syndrome), and synesthesia forcefully and memorably reveal the interpretive role of the brain. Technology may extend the senses marvelously, but the basic issue of appearance and reality remains. An electron microscope can render visual the width of a hydrogen atom, while the James Webb Space Telescope will be 100 times more powerful than the Hubble Telescope, which itself sees galaxies more than 13 billion light years away. The often counterintuitive theories of science, articulated on a strong armature of mathematics, are necessary to interpret and understand sensory stimuli. Conceptual frameworks enable perception. In the end, are we perceiving reality or understanding a biologically and culturally determined construction of the mind?

Philosophical dialogue may be used to develop students' understanding in an informed and personal manner. Students must express diverse points of view regarding a question or issue. One can frame this dialogue in different ways:

- As a question:
  - Do our senses deceive us?
  - Is perception knowledge?
  - To what extend may language extend or challenge perception?
  - Does art inform our perception?

- As a quotation from which students can extract and discuss a knowledge question:
  - "It has appeared that, if we take any common object of the sort that is supposed to be known by the senses, what the senses immediately tell us is not the truth about the object as it is apart from us, but only the truth about certain sense-data which, so far as we can see, depend upon the relations between us and the object. Thus what we directly see and feel is merely 'appearance', which we believe to be a sign of some 'reality' behind."—Bertrand Russell
  - "If the doors of perception were cleansed every thing would appear to man as it is, Infinite. For man has closed himself up, till he sees all things thro' narrow chinks of his cavern."—William Blake
  - "We must then grant that I could not even understand through the imagination what this piece of wax is, and that it is my mind alone which perceives it."—René Descartes (*Note.* Only use this quote if students have previously discussed the thought experiment concerning wax in class.)

- As a real-life situation from which the students extract and discuss a knowledge question:
  - In 1987 a 2-year-old girl swallowed many Tylenol samples, believing they were candy. She became extremely ill and was rushed to the hospital. Unexpectedly, the child recovered. The family attributed the cure to the intercession of a saint, and the Vatican deemed this incident a miracle in the canonization of Edith Stein in 1998.
  - Time crystals as a new form of matter were theorized in 2012 but were contested. In 2017, they were empirically discovered. A study later indicated that, in principle, time crystals might even be detected in more simple crystal-growing kits used by children.
  - Leonardo da Vinci's painting *Salvator Mundi* sold for $450 million in 2017. But the conservation report on the painting indicates the work has suffered significant paint losses. Images of the work stripped of the

repaints are dramatic. One eminent art historian attributed the work to a follower of Leonardo.

In each of these assignments, the students must dialectically explore a knowledge question, assigning different perspectives that collide within a conversation. The aim is not necessarily debate, but an enriching discussion.

THINKING WITH OTHERS

Imaginative philosophical dialogues allow students to explore ideas and are fun to write. They complement and enrich the dialogues in the classroom, and they provide a valid and challenging alternative to essays. Students are encouraged to look past the boundaries of their own convictions and arguments to take into account the views of others. Thinking is a social activity enriched by others. The philosophical dialogue expresses this social dynamic, reflecting how ideas surface and are shaped within a community. The ideal is not so much Auguste Rodin's *Thinker* contemplating in isolation (i.e., a brooding individual genius), but rather the free discussion of diverse people found in Raphael's *School of Athens*, in which Plato and Aristotle stand in the center of a community of inquiry.

CHAPTER 7

SOCRATIC METHODS

IN WHAT WAY SOCRATIC?
TO WHAT EXTENT SOCRATIC?

Make all preparations for a gale. Main tack and clew-garnet gone, what is to be done?

—*Practical Seamanship Examination*,
Naval Academy, June 1881

EXTEND AND CHALLENGE

If we take a step back, we can see that teaching through a Socratic adaptation very often begins with selecting an issue (or issues), then choosing a problem or a series of problems, and then formulating a series of questions to understand and solve the problem(s). Figure 8 outlines this process. To assemble a Socratic lesson, we must ask ourselves: What are the most important issues? What are the most complicated situations for those issues? What question sequence will guide the exploration of the situation as well as the analysis and evaluation of the issues? From these fundamental preliminary steps, the Socratic outline—never entirely binding—is composed.

Socrates conversed with a single person or a small group, and even in a small group, he engaged one person at a time. His conversations, to some extent, were like

DOI: 10.4324/9781003238089-8

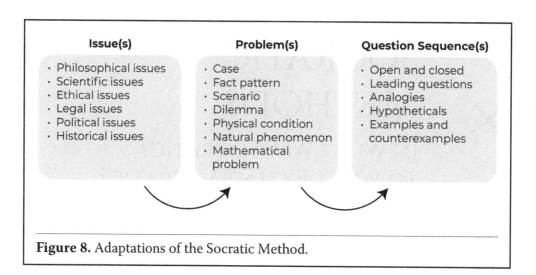

Issue(s)	Problem(s)	Question Sequence(s)
• Philosophical issues • Scientific issues • Ethical issues • Legal issues • Political issues • Historical issues	• Case • Fact pattern • Scenario • Dilemma • Physical condition • Natural phenomenon • Mathematical problem	• Open and closed • Leading questions • Analogies • Hypotheticals • Examples and counterexamples

Figure 8. Adaptations of the Socratic Method.

tutorial sessions. The contemporary classroom does not often permit such a narrow focus. For classroom teachers, the process of questioning more often involves meaningfully engaging the entire group.

Form follows function—the dictum of Henry Louis Sullivan, who was the father of the modern skyscraper—holds true for Socratic adaptations. When modified according to the knowledge domain and pedagogical purpose, the Socratic Method instills in students a model for critical thinking and problem solving. Animated with curiosity and skepticism, students use the Socratic Method to guide and test individual or collective reasoning and judgment. Rather than clinging to intuitive convictions or unexamined biases and assumptions, they can gain perspective and scrutinize ideas with other people. Students can turn the ideas in different directions, looking at them from other perspectives. Through careful shared analysis, students move from intuitive convictions to better understood conscious convictions or to the rejection of intuitions.

As Sylvius showed in the 17th century, an effective Socratic moderator guides a discussion or debate among the students (Jones, 1952; Parent, 2016). This is the Socratic adaptation used by Michael Sandel (2009), who teaches political philosophy at Harvard. Well-edited excerpts from his sessions are viewable online (see https://www.youtube.com/playlist?list=PL30C13C91CFFEFEA6). Sandel structures the class around well-selected problems of justice that can stimulate discussion, debate, and reflection. For instance, in one lesson he introduced Jeremy Bentham's utilitarianism (Harvard University, 2009). To test the concept, he presented a shocking late 19th-century legal case of cannibalism on the high seas with *The Queen v. Dudley and Stephens* (1884). An Australian barrister had purchased a yacht in England and required a crew to sail it to Australia. Four men were hired, with Dudley as the captain, and the trip began. However, after a few weeks, a storm in the Atlantic wrecked the yacht, compelling the four men to scurry onto a dinghy, carrying only two turnips and a sextant. Alone and drifting in the middle of the Atlantic Ocean, they survived on the two turnips and a sea turtle they managed to catch and kill. But each day was harder. After 8 days there was no more food or water. Two weeks after the wreck, the cabin boy, against the urgings of the others, drank ocean water and soon became extremely ill. For the experienced sailors, it was clear that he would die. Holding a notion of "the law of the high seas," Dudley and Stephens reasoned that in such a circumstance they were permitted to kill the young man so that they might survive. For them, it was a clear case of the death of one for survival of three. They drew lots, and Dudley killed the young man. Four days later they were rescued. Were the sailors right in their moral calculation? How does one condemn or justify the conduct of the sailors who cannibalized their crewmate? Sandel (Harvard University, 2009) skillfully moderated a small debate among the students, much as Sylvius did in Leiden in The Netherlands 350 years ago. (In the end the two men were condemned and sentenced to death, but they were later pardoned.)

Becoming a critical thinker means assimilating the model of curious, skeptical, and creative questioning by exploring many problems. The Socratic dialogue is interiorized. Socrates did not instruct teachers; he conversed with everyone. Young men assimilated (undoubtedly to differing extents) his skill in questioning. Problem-posing education permits students to become coinvestigators with the teacher. Perry (1970) suggested very well the transformative effect of an education in critical thinking. The student is invited and guided to think personally and to make well-founded personal commitments in a pluralistic world.

WHAT DOES A SOCRATIC CLASSROOM LOOK LIKE?

The Socratic Method is one among many teaching and learning strategies. It was not born within a classroom or auditorium. Its most natural and familiar context, as described by Plato and Xenophon, may be anywhere within the polis. In the best of circumstances, students first learn about Socrates and his method before engaging with the Socratic Method. Students should have read and discussed excerpts from Plato and Xenophon. They should understand the purpose and form of Socratic questioning. Then, they can assimilate the skills in questioning to deconstruct a problem, perceive the issues, and analyze and evaluate the concepts, arguments, assumptions, consequences, and implications. Ideally this familiarization takes place in conversation, with the students thinking aloud and interacting in their collective analysis and evaluation.

The classroom experience will never mirror the literary performances of Plato and Xenophon. It is likely that the well-designed written sequences of questions in those ancient sources, which are useful as models, only approximate the general attributes and tone of the inquiry Socrates used. The actual interactions with Socrates most likely were rougher, marked by repetitions, clarifications, pauses for indecision, pauses for reflection, unsure answers, and laughter. Socrates was brilliant, yes, but he was also gregarious, earthy, irreverent, and witty, and all of those qualities must have moved through his conversations, delighting listeners and attracting followers in a broad public space. Socrates offered far more than a demanding lesson with a professor in a classroom. Similar to what Crossan (2012) termed "challenge parables," the Socratic Method is participatory pedagogy articulated with personally challenging conceptual problems, cases, and questions. Literary performances are tidy in comparison.

In his lecture on legal Socratic Method (one of the best texts on the legal variation), Areeda (1996) articulated a short list of what the Socratic Method is *not*. Areeda noted that the Socratic Method is not the case method in itself, the simple recitation of an assignment, an antiphonal catechism or information drill, an opinion survey, the posing of a big question that may invite unprepared student speeches, or a perfunctory pause in the lecture. Moreover, the Socratic Method is not simply a vehicle for communicating information.

One might extend the list a little further. The Socratic Method is not the quick rephrasing of a student's question, which is then posed to the student or the group. Nor is the Socratic Method the amplification or clarification of the student's point, sharpening the idea, supplying a better example, and speaking at greater length in a mini-lecture (a common temptation). It is not a subtle (or not-so-subtle) form of one-upmanship. It is not taking refuge in the ample repertoire of strategies to avoid answering questions, as politicians might by ignoring the question, questioning the question, or attacking the question (Bull & Mayer, 1993). Nor is it an hour of Q and A.

A Socratic classroom explores ill-structured problems that require Kahneman's (2011) System 2 Thinking. It proceeds (as Socrates did) by sequences of such problems. Arguably, this is the perfect strategy for stimulating progression beyond the phased prereflective reasoning that is dependent upon authority (King & Kitchener, 1994, 2002).

Ideally, in the Socratic classroom *everyone becomes Socrates* to a certain extent. Curiosity and skepticism animate the discussion that may have moments of civil debate and, when appropriate, moments of maieutic clarification or extension. The students understand the nature and limits of the basic questions and issues they explore. They can differentiate and discern the qualities of a scientific question, a historical question, an ethical question, a psychological question, a religious question, a philosophical question, a legal question, a political question, etc. Each domain appeals to a slightly different form of Socratic Method.

THE VALUE OF PHILOSOPHY IN SCHOOLS

Karl Jaspers (1951/1964) wrote, "There is no escape from philosophy" (p. 12). However, although philosophy is present in some American schools, it is not widely taught across the nation. There have been informed and admirable efforts at presenting philosophy for children, as Lipman (1984) began, but there is no national or state curriculum or a series of standards for philosophy in secondary schools. Still, when students consider ethical and political issues in civics or American history, or personal issues concerning happiness, friendship, and love in literature, they are encountering philosophical issues—problems that do not have a historical or literary solution. Within science classes, when students learn how human beings can now alter the basic codes of life, they encounter a philosophical issue: Is it right to do so, and to what extent? How does one reason about these issues? Philosophical issues are present in every curriculum, and yet there is not an organized, concentrated, and sustained effort to teach philosophical thinking. Indeed, for some teachers who are aware that there is not an empirical or otherwise objective answer to philosophical questions, it may seem correct not to point out the controversial issues in class and thus avoid philosophical disagreements that may at first appear difficult to manage. In balancing pragmatic interests for college preparation, it may seem deceptively easy for teachers and students to jettison philosophy.

Philosophy is more commonly taught in secondary schools in Europe, where many countries have a national curriculum in philosophy (United Nations Educational, Scientific and Cultural Organization, 2007). Basically, there are three overlapping approaches to the subject: by chronology, by branch, or by theme. The first approach surveys philosophers and their ideas, from Thales in Ancient Greece to the present, often with more treatment of salient national figures. The second approach isolates an area of philosophy (e.g., ethics, epistemology, logic, aesthetics) and looks at the major ideas and questions according to that framework. The third approach, followed in France, selects larger themes (e.g., culture, reason and reality, politics, morality) as well as individual topics with issues (e.g., perception, language, interpretation, justice and law, freedom). The national curriculum also suggests a list of possible philosophical authors. The French approach emphasizes learning to think philosophically to form citizens who can reason responsibly at the level of principle. Each year in June, France holds national examinations, and philosophy is always the first examination. The 4-hour essay topics are challenging. In 2018, the questions included the following: Does culture make us more human? Can one renounce truth? Is all truth definitive? Can one be insensitive to art? Is it necessary to experience injustice to know what is just? (Le Parisien Etudíant, 2018).

A fourth and uniquely hybrid approach to teaching philosophy can be seen in the International Baccalaureate (IB), a demanding program that is increasingly popular in the United States, which offers a short compulsory course in the Theory of Knowledge (TOK). During the 1960s, when a group of international educators conceived and organized the first iteration of the IB program, there was a desire for a philosophy course but an awareness that there were different approaches to the subject in the Anglo-Saxon and French education systems (Hill, 2010). The International Baccalaureate compromised and decided to focus on one branch: explanations of knowledge and how knowledge is constructed. Peterson (1972) explained that by making the principles of knowledge construction explicit, IB students would enter university not simply knowing facts from their subject classes, but also knowing how to think mathematically, historically, scientifically, ethically, and aesthetically, and having some awareness of how these ways of thinking interrelate. The French philosopher Dina Dreyfus, whose life was rather adventurous (she accompanied her husband Claude Levi Strauss to South America in the 1930s and was an active member of the French Resistance during World War II), wrote the first Theory of Knowledge syllabus (Hill, 2010). Although altered over the decades, the ambitious TOK course maintains a French philosophical approach to learning how to think about knowledge within eight different areas and through eight different ways of knowing. Its aim is for students to perceive knowledge questions and to have some awareness of how to approach them. Like the French program, it requires students to write an argumentative essay on a prescribed title. But, having little required historical philosophical content and a limited number of hours over two years, this hybrid approach is more limited as an experience of learning philosophy.

There are, therefore, different options for creating a philosophy course in secondary schools. Courses can be presented by branch, by chronology, or by theme. In all of these approaches, students encounter the issues and ideas that give meaning and form to their lives. In philosophy courses framed with Socratic conversations, rather than arguing and rather than learning rote facts, students learn respectful dialogue and debate about issues that cannot be avoided in our local and larger community. Are there human rights? Is health care a right? Is housing a right? Should an algorithm be used for criminal sentencing? Is a social score for citizens, as China has begun implementing, helpful for society? Is truth just an opinion? How do we distinguish the substance from the "humbug" (to use Black's [1982] term)? How do we reason about such questions?

Philosophy gives us the content and the means for such discussions in a community. If philosophy is removed from or neglected in schools, the result is simply vocational or technical training, which is useful but neglects fundamental issues in which we have a stake. If students have not developed the conceptual tools to analyze and evaluate meaning according to explicit (and discussable) criteria, it is more tempting for them to ignore or shout down an opposing point of view. Philosophical conversation is free speech in a wide sense.

Problem-centered Socratic education, which focuses concepts and issues, equips students for the challenges of the contemporary pace of life in a pluralistic community. Socratic questioning models and instills a mode of approaching the world whose challenges are not limited to keeping up with swiftly changing knowledge.

REFERENCES

Abel, R. (1976). *Man is the measure: A cordial invitation to the central problems of philosophy.* New York, NY: Free Press.

Abrams, J. R. (2015). Reframing the Socratic Method. *Journal of Legal Education, 64,* 562–585.

Adams, J. (1904). *Primer on teaching, with special reference to Sunday school work.* Edinburgh, Scotland: Clark.

Ames, J. B. (1874a). Examination for civil procedure. In C. W. Sever (Ed.), *The Harvard University catalogue. 1874–1875* (pp. 282–283). Cambridge, MA: Harvard University Press.

Ames, J. B. (1874b). Examination for contracts. In C. W. Sever (Ed.), *The Harvard University catalogue. 1874–1875* (pp. 278–279). Cambridge, MA: Harvard University Press.

Ames, J. B. (1876a). Examination for contracts. In C. W. Sever (Ed.), *The Harvard University catalogue. 1876–1877* (pp. 275–276). Cambridge, MA: Harvard University Press.

Ames, J. B. (1876b). Examination for torts. In C. W. Sever (Ed.), *The Harvard University catalogue. 1876–1877* (pp. 276–277). Cambridge, MA: Harvard University Press.

Arbesman, S. (2012a). *The half-life of facts: Sam Arbesman at TEDxKC* [Video file]. Retrieved from https://www.youtube.com/watch?v=GaxYnvd7YAM

Arbesman, S. (2012b). *The half-life of facts: Why everything we know has an expiration date.* New York, NY: Penguin.

Areeda, P. E. (1996). The Socratic Method (SM) (Lecture at Puget Sound, 1/31/90). *Harvard Law Review, 119,* 911–922.

Baggini, J. (2003). *Making sense: Philosophy behind the headlines.* Oxford, England: Oxford University Press.

Baggini, J., & Fosl, P. S. (2010). *The philosopher's toolkit. A compendium of philosophical concepts and methods* (2nd ed.). Hoboken, NJ: Wiley-Blackwell.

Baggini, J., & Krauss, L. (2012). Philosophy v science: Which can answer the big questions of life? *The Guardian.* Retrieved from https://www.theguardian.com/science/2012/sep/09/science-philosophy-debate-julian-baggini-lawrence-krauss

Bensley, D. A. (2011). Rules for reasoning revisited: Toward a scientific conception of critical thinking. In C. P. Horvath & J. M. Forte (Eds.), *Critical thinking* (pp. 1–35). Hauppauge, NY: Nova Science.

Black, M. (1946). *Critical thinking. An introduction to logic and scientific method.* New York, NY: Prentice-Hall.

Black, M. (1982). The prevalence of humbug. *Philosophic Exchange, 13*(1), 1–23.

Blakemore, S.-J. (2012). *The mysterious workings of the adolescent brain* [Video file]. Retrieved from https://www.ted.com/talks/sarah_jayne_blakemore_the_mysterious_workings_of_the_adolescent_brain

Blakemore, S.-J., & Frith, U. (2005). *The learning brain: Lessons for education.* Malden, MA: Wiley-Blackwell.

Blatner, A. (2000). *Foundations of psychodrama: History, drama, and practice* (4th ed.). New York, NY: Springer.

Bloom, B. (Ed.). (1956). *Taxonomy of educational objectives: The classification of educational goals. Handbook I: Cognitive domain.* New York, NY: Longmans Green.

Bode, B. H. (1927). *Modern educational theories.* New York, NY: Macmillan.

Brancati, F. L. (1989). The art of pimping. *The Journal of the American Medical Association, 262,* 89–90.

Brancusi v. United States, 54 Treas. Dec. 428. (Cust Ct. 1928).

Briggs, H. (2018). First monkey clones created in Chinese laboratory. *BBC News.* Retrieved from https://www.bbc.com/news/health-42809445

Brightland, J. (1759). *A grammar of the English tongue, with the arts of logick, rhetorick, poetry, &c., illustrated with useful notes giving the grounds and reasons of grammar in general, the whole making a compleat system of an English education* (8th ed.). London, England: Rivington and Fletcher.

The British Medical Journal. (1886, February 26). Clinical teaching and clinical teachers. *The British Medical Journal, 1*(1312), 353–354.

Brothers of the Christian Schools. (1912). *The catechist's manual. Brief course* (3rd ed.). Philadelphia, PA: McVey.

Brown, J. R., & Fehige, Y. (2014). Thought experiments. *Stanford Encyclopedia of Philosophy.* Retrieved from https://plato.stanford.edu/entries/thought-experiment

Browne, M. N., & Keeley, S. M. (2015). *Asking the right questions: A guide to critical thinking* (11th ed.). Englewood Cliffs, NJ: Prentice-Hall.

Bull, P., & Mayer, K. (1993). How not to answer questions in political interviews. *Political Psychology, 14,* 651–666.

Cambridge Assessment Admissions Testing. (2019). *Thinking Skills Assessment (TSA).* Retrieved from https://www.admissionstesting.org/for-test-takers/thinking-skills-assessment

Carlson, E. R. (2017). Medical pimping versus the Socratic Method of teaching. *The Journal of Oral and Maxillofacial Surgery, 75*(1), 3–5.

Christensen, C. R., Garvin, D. A., & Sweet, A. (Eds.). (1991). *Education for judgment: The artistry of discussion leadership.* Boston, MA: Harvard Business School.

Clark, E. E. (1992). *Legal education and professional development—An educational continuum. Report of the task force on law schools and the profession: Narrowing the gap.* Chicago, IL: American Bar Association.

Conant, J. B. (1964). *Two modes of thought. My encounters with science and education.* New York, NY: Trident Press.

Coquillette, D. R., & Kimball, B. A. (2015). *On the battlefield of merit: Harvard Law School, the first century.* Cambridge, MA: Harvard University Press.

Crossan, J. D. (2012). *The power of parable: How fiction by Jesus became fiction about Jesus.* New York, NY: HarperCollins.

CTLStanford. (2013). *The Socratic Method: What it is and how to use it in the classroom* [Video file]. Retrieved from https://www.youtube.com/watch?v=Kr_NtXFskQw

CTLStanford. (2015). *The power and pitfalls of the Socratic Method in teaching* [Video file]. Retrieved from https://www.youtube.com/watch?v=CXX75ioEJLQ

Cuban, L. (1993). *How teachers taught: Constancy and change in American classrooms, 1890–1990* (2nd ed.). New York, NY: Teachers College Press.

Cunningham, A. S., Blatt, S. D., Fuller, P. G., & Weinberger, H. L. (1999). The art of precepting: Socrates or Aunt Minnie? *Archives of Pediatrics and Adolescent Medicine, 153,* 114–116.

Dalham, F. (1762). *De ratione recte cogitandi, loquendi et intelligendi libri III* [Three books on the method of correctly reasoning, speaking, and understanding]. Augsburg, Germany: Rieger.

Dennett, D. C. (2013). *Intuition pumps and other tools for thinking.* New York, NY: Norton.

Donham, W. B. (1922). Business teaching by the case system. *American Economic Review, 12,* 53–65.

Drucker, P. F. (1999). Knowledge-worker productivity: The biggest challenge. *California Management Review, 41*(2), 79–94.

Duke, N. K., Pearson, P. D., Strachan, S. L., & Billman, A. K. (2011). Essential elements of fostering and teaching reading comprehension. In S. J. Samuels & A. E. Farstrup (Eds.), *What research has to say about reading instruction* (4th ed., pp. 51–93). Newark, DE: International Reading Association.

Durkin, M. (1993). *Thinking through class discussion: The Hilda Taba approach.* Lancaster, PA: R&L Education.

Engelman, R. (2009). *Friendlyvision : Fred Friendly and the rise and fall of television journalism.* New York, NY: Columbia University Press.

Ennis, R. H. (1958). An appraisal of the Watson-Glaser critical thinking appraisal. *Journal of Educational Research, 52,* 155–158.

Ennis, R. H. (1993). Critical thinking assessment. *Theory Into Practice, 32,* 179–186.

Examination of James Madden. (1833). *The Lancet, 20,* 669–670.

Foot, P. (1967). The problem of abortion and the doctrine of double effect. *Oxford Review, 5,* 5–15.

Freire, P. (1996). *Pedagogy of the oppressed.* London, England: Penguin.

Gallagher, A. (Ed.). (1979). *The methods book: Strategies for law-focused education.* Chicago, IL: Law in American Society Foundation.

Gallagher, E. (2008). *Equal rights to the curriculum: Many languages, one message.* Clevedon, England: Multilingual Matters.

Gewirtz, P. (1982). The jurisprudence of hypotheticals. *Journal of Legal Education, 32,* 120–126.

Gilligan, C., Kegan, R., & Sizer, T. (1999). Memorial minute: William Graves Perry, Jr. *The Harvard University Gazette.*

Glaser, E. M. (1941). *An experiment in the development of critical thinking.* New York, NY: Teachers College, Columbia University.

Gordon, B. R. (1993). Edward Maynard Glaser, Ph.D. *Consulting Psychology Journal: Practice and Research, 45,* 76–77.

Gordon, B. R. (1994). Edward Maynard Glaser (1911–1993): Obituary. *American Psychologist, 49,* 755.

Gorvine, H. (1970). Teaching history through role playing. *The History Teacher, 3*(4), 7–20.

Gray, J. C. (1888). Cases and treatises. *The American Law Review, 22,* 756–764.

Greco, J. (2010a). *The commandments of moderating a panel, parts 1–2: The basic basics* [Web log post]. Retrieved from https://goodquestionconsulting.com/2010/09/21/the-ten-commandments-of-moderating-a-panel-parts-1-2-the-basic-basics

Greco, J. (2010b). *The commandments of moderating, part 3: Hard questions.* Retrieved from https://goodquestionconsulting.com/2010/09/21/the-ten-commandments-of-moderating-part-3-hard-questions

Greco, J. (2010c). *The commandments of moderating, part 4: Conversations* [Web log post]. Retrieved from https://goodquestionconsulting.com/2010/09/30/the-ten-commandments-of-moderating-part-4-conversations

Greco, J. (2010d). *The commandments of moderating, part 5: Paint pictures.* Retrieved from https://goodquestionconsulting.com/2010/10/08/the-ten-commandments-of-moderating-part-5-paint-pictures

Greco, J. (2010e). *My favorite question* [Web log post]. Retrieved from https://goodquestionconsulting.com/2010/05/28/my-favorite-question

Greco, J. (2010f). *Panelists just say no* [Web log post]. Retrieved from https://goodquestionconsulting.com/2010/09/02/panelists-just-say-no

Greco, J. (2011). *The commandments of moderating, part 6: Prepare, but don't overprepare, panelists and part 7: Directing traffic* [Web log post]. Retrieved from https://goodquestionconsulting.com/2011/01/02/the-ten-commandments-of-moderating-part-6-prepare-but-dont-overprepare-panelists

Greco, J. (2017). *The commandments of moderating, part 8–10: Listen, listen, listen.* Retrieved from https://goodquestionconsulting.com/2017/01/13/the-commandments-of-moderating-part-7-its-not-about-you

Groarke, L. (2017). Informal logic. *Stanford Encyclopedia of Philosophy.* Retrieved from https://plato.stanford.edu/archives/spr2017/entries/logic-informal

Hartshorne, T. L. (1986). Modernism on trial: C. Brancusi v. United States (1928). *Journal of American Studies, 20,* 93–104.

Harvard University. (2009). *Justice: What's the right thing to do? Episode 1: The moral side of murder* [Video file]. Retrieved from https://www.youtube.com/watch?v=kBdfcR-8hEY&t=1862s.

Herbert, G. (1652). *A priest to the temple, or the country parson.* London, England: Maxey.

Herreid, C. F. (Ed.). (2007). *Start with a story. The case study method of teaching college science.* Arlington, VA: National Science Teachers Association.

Hill, I. (2010). The International Baccalaureate: Pioneering in education. In M. Hayden (Ed.), *The international schools journal compendium* (Vol. IV). Woodbridge, England: John Catt Educational.

Holyoak, K. J., & Morrison, R. G. (Eds.). (2005). *The Cambridge handbook of thinking and reasoning.* New York, NY: Cambridge University Press.

Holyoak, K. J., & Morrison, R .G. (Eds.). (2012). *The Oxford handbook of thinking and reasoning.* New York, NY: Oxford University Press.

Hudson, M. (2003). Acting out muscle contraction. *American Biology Teacher, 65,* 128–132.

Hull, G. (1997). The influence of Herman Boerhaave. *Journal of the Royal Society of Medicine, 90,* 512–514.

Jaspers, K. (1964). *Way to wisdom: An introduction to philosophy.* (R. Manheim, Trans.). London, England: Yale University Press. (Original work published 1951)

Jensen, E. (2005). *Teaching with the brain in mind* (2nd ed.). Alexandria, VA: Association for Supervision and Curriculum Development.

Johnston-Wilder, S., Lee, C., & Pimm, D. (2017). *Learning to teach mathematics in the secondary school: A companion to school experience* (4th ed.). London, England: Routledge.

Jones, A. M. (1952). Medical progress and medical education. *The British Medical Journal, 2,* 466–469.

Jones, A. S. (1987). Television; Fred Friendly enjoys putting talking heads on the hot seat. *The New York Times.* Retrieved from https://www.nytimes.com/1987/02/01/arts/television-fred-friendly-enjoys-putting-talking-heads-on-the-hot-seat.html

Kahneman, D. (2011). *Thinking fast and slow.* New York, NY: Farrar, Straus and Giroux.

Kant, I. (2007). *Lectures on pedagogy.* In R. B. Louden & G. Zöller (Eds.), *Anthropology, history, and education* (pp. 434–485). Cambridge, England: Cambridge University Press. (Original work published 1803)

Katz, H. E., & O'Neill, K. F. (2009). *Strategies and techniques of law school teaching: A primer for new (and not so new) professors.* Cambridge, MA: Aspen.

Kelley, D. (2014). *The art of reasoning: An introduction to logic and critical thinking* (4th ed.). New York, NY: Norton.

Kimball, B. A. (2009). *The inception of modern professional education: C. C. Langdell, 1826–1906.* Chapel Hill: The University of North Carolina Press.

King, P. M., & Kitchener, K. S. (1994). *Developing reflective judgment: Understanding and promoting intellectual growth and critical thinking in adolescents and adults.* San Francisco, CA: Jossey-Bass.

King, P. M., & Kitchener, K. S. (2002). The reflective judgment model: Twenty years of research on epistemic cognition. In B. K. Hofer & P.R. Pintrich (Eds.), *Personal epistemology: The psychology of beliefs about knowledge and knowing* (pp. 37–61). London, England: Routledge.

Korzybski, A. (1958). *Science and sanity: An introduction to non-Aristotelian systems and general semantics* (5th ed.). New York, NY: Institute of General Semantics.

Kost, A., & Chen, F. M. (2015). Socrates was not a pimp: Changing the paradigm of questioning in medical education. *Academic Medicine, 90,* 20–24.

Kuhn, T. (1962). *The structure of scientific revolutions.* Chicago, IL: University of Chicago Press.

Langdell, C. C. (1871). *A selection of cases on the law of contracts with references and citations.* Boston, MA: Little, Brown.

Langdell, C. C. (1873). Examination for contracts. In C. W. Sever (Ed.), *The Harvard University catalogue. 1872–1873* (pp. 303–304). Cambridge, England: Harvard University Press.

Langdell, C. C. (1887). Professor Langdell's address. In J. Winsor (Ed.), *A record of the commemoration, November fifth to eighth, 1886, on the two hundred and fiftieth anniversary of the founding of Harvard College* (pp. 84–89). Cambridge, MA: Wilson and Son.

Law, S. (2003). *The philosophy gym: 25 short adventures in thinking.* New York, NY: St. Martin's Press.

Le Clerc, J. (1700). *Logica sive ars ratiocinandi* [Logic or the art of reasoning]. In *Opera Philosophica in Quatuor Volumina Digesta* (Vol. 1). Amsterdam, Netherlands: Georgium Gallet.

Le Parisien Etudíant. (2018). *Bac 2018: Les sujets complets de philosophie* [Complete topics of philosophy]. Retrieved from https://etudiant.aujourdhui.fr/etudiant/info/bac-2018-les-sujets-de-philosophie.html

Lepaulle, P. (1920). Le système du "Case" et la méthode Socratique dans les Ecoles de droit américain [The case system and the Socratic method in American law schools]. *Revue internationale de l'enseignement, 74,* 161–183.

Lipman, M. (1984). The cultivation of reasoning through philosophy. *Educational Leadership, 42*(1), 51–56.

Lipman, M. (1988a). Critical thinking: What can it be. *Educational Leadership, 46*(1), 38–43.

Lipman, M. (1988b). *Philosophy goes to school.* Philadelphia, PA: Temple University Press.

Lode, E. (1999). Slippery slope arguments and legal reasoning. *California Law Review, 87,* 1469–1543.

Masterpiece Cakeshop v. Colorado Civil Rights Commission, 138 S. Ct. 1719 (2017).

McLellan, J. A., & Dewey, J. (1890). *Applied psychology. An introduction to the principles and practice of education.* Boston, MA: Educational Publishing Company.

Medawar, P. (1996). *The strange case of the spotted mice and other classic essays on science.* Oxford, England: Oxford University Press.

Medicine and the Media. (1980). *The British Medical Journal, 280,* 556–557.

Meyerson, M. I. (1985, September/October). The incredible thinking heads. *Channels,* 35–36.

Miller, A. R. (1982). *Miller's court.* Boston, MA: Houghton Mifflin Harcourt.

Moore, B. N., & Parker, R. (2016). *Critical thinking* (12th ed.). New York, NY: McGraw-Hill Education.

Mortier, R. (2002). Dialogue. In M. Delon (Ed.), *Encyclopedia of the Enlightenment* (Vol. 1, pp. 378–386). London, England: Routledge.

Murdoch, I. (1986). *Acastos: Two platonic dialogues.* New York, NY: Penguin.

National Center for Education Statistics. (2018). *English language learners in public schools.* Retrieved from https://nces.ed.gov/programs/coe/indicator_cgf.asp

National Research Council. (2012). *A framework for K–12 science education: Practices, crosscutting concepts, and core ideas.* Washington, DC: The National Academies Press.

Neher, J. O., Gordon, K. C., Meyer, B., & Stevens, N. (1992). A five-step 'microskills' model of clinical teaching. *Journal of the American Board of Family Medicine, 5,* 419–424.

NGSS Lead States. (2013). *Next generation science standards: For states, by states.* Washington, DC: The National Academies Press.

The Nobel Foundation. (2002). *Press release: The Sveriges Riksbank Prize in Economic Sciences in memory of Alfred Nobel 2002.* Retrieved from https://www.nobel prize.org/prizes/economic-sciences/2002/press-release

Novak, J. D., & Gowin, D. B. (1984). *Learning how to learn.* New York, NY: Cambridge University Press.

Nussbaum, M. (2010). *Not for profit: Why democracy needs the humanities.* Princeton, NJ: Princeton University Press.

Organisation for Economic Co-operation and Development. (2007). *Understanding the brain: The birth of a learning science.* Paris, France: Author.

Parent, A. (2016). Franciscus Sylvius on clinical teaching, iatrochemistry and brain anatomy. *Canadian Journal of Neurological Sciences, 43,* 596–603.

Paul, R. (2005). The state of critical thinking today. *New Directions for Community Colleges, 130,* 27–38.

Paul, R., & Elder, L. (2007a). Critical thinking: the art of Socratic questioning. *Journal of Developmental Education, 31*(1), 36–37.

Paul, R., & Elder, L. (2007b). Critical thinking: the art of Socratic questioning, Part II. *Journal of Developmental Education, 32*(2), 32–33.

Pearson, P. D., & Gallagher, M. C. (1983). The instruction of reading comprehension. *Contemporary Educational Psychology, 8,* 317–344.

Perry, J. (1978). *A dialogue on personal identity and immortality.* Indianapolis, IN: Hackett.

Perry, W. G. (1970). *Forms of intellectual and ethical development in the college year.* Cambridge, MA: Harvard University Press.

Peterson, A. D. C. (1972). *The International Baccalaureate. An experiment in international education.* London, England: Harrap.

Pierson v. Post, 3 Cai. R. 175, 2 Am. Dec. 264 (1805).

Pólya, G. (1963). On learning, teaching, and learning teaching. *The American Mathematical Monthly, 70,* 605–619

Pólya, G. (2014). *How to solve it: A new aspect of mathematical method* (4th ed.). Princeton, NJ: Princeton University Press.

The Queen v. Dudley and Stephens, 14 QBD 273 DC (1884).

Randak, S. (1990). Role-playing in the classroom. *American Biology Teacher, 52,* 439–442.

Repanich, J. (2019). Japan's sushi king just paid a record-smashing $3 million for one bluefin tuna. *Robb Report*. Retrieved from https://robbreport.com/food-drink/dining/japan-bluefin-tuna-auction-record-smashed-2837623

Reich, R. (2003). The Socratic Method: What it is and how to use it in the classroom. *Speaking of Teaching: The Stanford Newsletter on Teaching, 13*(1), 1–4.

Reifler, D. R. (2015). The pedagogy of pimping. Educational rigor or mistreatment. *The Journal of the American Medical Association, 314*, 2355–2356.

Rissland, E. L. (1983). Examples in legal reasoning: Legal hypotheticals. In A. Bundy (Ed.), *Proceedings of the 8th International Joint Conference on Artificial Intelligence* (pp. 90–93). Karlsruhe, West Germany: Kaufmann.

Sandel, M. J. (2009). *Justice: What's the right thing to do?* New York, NY: Farrar, Straus and Giroux.

Schaeffer, N. C. (1896). Teaching pupils to think. *Journal of Education, 43*, 343–345.

Schick, T., & Vaughn, L. (2014). *How to think about weird things: Critical thinking for a new age* (7th ed.). New York, NY: McGraw-Hill.

Schwartz, M. H., Hess, G. F., & Sparrow, S. M. (2013). *What the best law teachers do.* Cambridge, MA: Harvard University Press.

Simon, K. (Director). (1966). *Let us teach guessing* [Motion picture]. United States: Mathematical Association of America.

The Socratic Method in Clinical Teaching. (1888). *The Lancet, 131*, 834–835.

Solum, L. B. (2015). *Legal theory lexicon 003: Hypotheticals* [Web log post]. Retrieved from https://lsolum.typepad.com/legal_theory_lexicon/2003/09/legal_theory_le.html

Stamper, W. R. (1973). Role-playing in the biology classroom. *The American Biology Teacher, 35*, 251–253, 295.

Sternberg, P., & Garcia, A. (2000). *Sociodrama: Who's in your shoes?* (2nd ed.). Westport, CT: Praeger.

Sternberg, R. J. (1986). *Critical thinking: Its nature, measurement, and improvement.* Washington, DC: National Institute of Education.

Sternberg, R. L., & Grigorenko, E. L. (2004). Successful intelligence in the classroom. *Theory Into Practice, 43*, 274–280.

Stoddard, H. A., & O'Dell, D. V. (2016). Would Socrates have actually used the 'Socratic Method' for clinical teaching? *Journal of General Internal Medicine, 31*, 1092–1096.

Sullivan, W. M., Colby, A., Wegner, J. W., Bond, L., & Shulman, L. S. (2007). *Educating lawyers: Preparation for the profession of law.* San Francisco, CA: Jossey-Bass.

Sutherland, A. E. (1957). La formation du juriste américain [The formation of the American lawyer]. *Revue Internationale de Droit Compare, 9*, 550–561.

Swatridge, C. (2014). *The Oxford Guide to effective argument and critical thinking.* Oxford, England: Oxford University Press.

Thayer, V. T. (1928). *The passing of the recitation.* New York, NY: Heath.

Thomas, W. P., & Collier, V. P. (1997). *School effectiveness for language minority students. Resource Collection Series, No. 9.* Washington, DC: National Clearinghouse for Bilingual Education.

Thomas, W. P., & Collier, V. P. (2002). *A national study of school effectiveness for language minority students' long-term academic achievement. Final Report: Project 1.1.* University of California, Santa Cruz: Center for Research, Education, Diversity and Excellence.

Thompson, J. F. (1978). *Using role-playing in the classroom.* Bloomington, IN: Phi Delta Kappa Educational Foundation.

Tozzi, M. (1999). *Penser par soi-même, Initiation à la philosophie* [Think for yourself: An initiation to philosophy] (4th ed.). Lyon, France: Chronique Sociale.

Turow, S. (1977). *One L: The turbulent true story of a first year at Harvard Law School.* New York, NY: Farrar, Straus and Giroux.

Tyler, W. S. (1859). A model teacher. *The Massachusetts Teacher, 12,* 462–467.

Tyler, W. S. (1867). Socrates as a teacher. In *The lectures delivered before the American Institute of Instruction at Burlington, Vermont, August, 1866* (pp. 139–194). Boston, MA: Committee of Publication.

Understanding Science. (n.d.). *The real process of science.* Retrieved from https://undsci.berkeley.edu/article/howscienceworks_02

United Nations Educational, Scientific and Cultural Organization. (2007). *Philosophy, a school of freedom: Teaching philosophy and learning to philosophize: Status and prospects.* Paris, France: Author.

United States v. Olivotti & Co., 7 Ct. Cust. App. 46 (1916).

Voltaire. (1765). Dialogue du chapon et de la poularde [Dialogue of the capon and the hen]. In *Nouveaux mélanges philosophiques, historiques, critiques, etc.: Troisième partie* (pp. 179–186). Geneva, Switzerland: Cramer.

Wambaugh, E. (1906). Professor Langdell: A view of his career. *Harvard Law Review, 20,* 1–4.

Warburton, N. (2008). *M. M. McCabe on Socratic Method* [Audio podcast]. Retrieved from https://philosophybites.com/2008/08/mm-mccabe-on-so.html

Warburton, N. (2013). *Philosophy: The basics* (5th ed.). London, England: Routledge.

Warren, E. H. (1942). *Spartan education.* Boston, MA: Houghton Mifflin Harcourt.

Watts, I. (1743). *The improvement of the mind; Or, a supplement to the art of logick, containing a variety of remarks and rules for the attainment and communication of useful knowledge in religion, in the sciences, and in common life.* London, England: James Brackstone.

Wear, D., Kokinova, M., Keck-McNulty, C., & Aultman, J. (2005). Pimping: Perspectives of 4th year medical students. *Teaching and Learning in Medicine, 17,* 184–191.

Wilberding, E. (2014). *Teach like Socrates: Guiding Socratic dialogues and discussions in the classroom.* Waco, TX: Prufrock Press.

Williams, S. M. (1992). Putting case-based instruction into context: Examples from legal and medical education. *The Journal of the Learning Sciences, 2,* 367–427.

Wilson, J. M. (1867). On teaching natural science in schools. In F. W. Farrar (Ed.), *Essays on a liberal education* (pp. 241–291). London, England: MacMillan.

Withington, E. T. (1894). *Medical history from the earliest times. A popular history of the healing art.* London, England: The Scientific Press.

Wolpaw, T. M, Wolpaw, D. R., & Papp, K. K. (2003). SNAPPS: A learner-centered model for outpatient education. *Academic Medicine, 78,* 893–898.

Wolpert, L. (1992). *The unnatural nature of science: Why science does not make (common) sense.* Cambridge, MA: Harvard University Press.

Wyn, M. A., & Stegink, S. J. (2000). Role-playing mitosis. *American Biology Teacher, 62,* 378–381.

APPENDIX

SAMPLE LESSON PLAN

In this sample lesson, we examine "What is art?"—a vexing question that permits a variety of answers and calls attention to how knowledge is constructed by communities. The basis of the discussion is the case of *Brancusi v. United States* (1928).

Defining art, as we saw in the case of *Masterpiece Cakeshop v. Colorado Civil Rights Commission*, is a notoriously thorny problem. What is acceptable to one audience may be deemed unacceptable to another. One may find an example that will fit the definition of art but is not generally accepted as a work, or one may find an example that does not fit the definition but is generally accepted as a work of art. The issue is an intersection of other delicate and central issues that include freedom of speech, freedom of exercise of religion, and freedom from discrimination on the basis of race, religion, gender, or sexual orientation. In a pluralistic society, the potential for controversy of different kinds is ever present.

The teacher may select from different examples of controversial art, each regarding the problem from a different angle. For instance, Dadaist Marcel Duchamp's *Fountain* (1917) ignites lively discussion on what may be considered a work of art. Chris Ofili's *Holy Virgin Mary* (1996) presents the problem in an intense manner with a work of sacred art. Performance art adventurously challenges the conventions of art. Land art, such as Maya Lin's deeply moving *Vietnam Veterans Memorial* (1981), also stimulates discussion. Video installations by artists such as Bill Viola also spark reflection and discussion in an image-dominated culture.

Landmark legal cases throw into relief some of the contours of the problem. The controversy surrounding Richard Serra's *Tilted Arc* (1981) highlights the nature and relationship of artist, public artwork, site, and audience. Decades before this, Constantin Brancusi's work was the subject of controversy in the courts, and it is this case that will be the center of this lesson. In formulating hypothetical (what if) questions, we will focus on the artist, the artwork, the audience, and the place.

In 1926, Marcel Duchamp curated an exhibition in New York for the Romanian sculptor Constantin Brancusi, who had studied art in Paris, worked briefly in the studio of Auguste Rodin in 1907, and was an acknowledged abstract sculptor. When Brancusi's work arrived at the port in New York, there was disagreement about whether it constituted art (Hartshorne, 1986). A customs official, applying the standards of the Fordney–McCumber Tariff Act of 1922, did not agree that the abstract work *Bird in Space* was art. He exacted a tariff of 40% of the value of the metal. An artwork would have been free of tariff. Supported by Edward Steichen and other wealthy members of the New York art world, Brancusi took the issue to the courts.

The legal system worked with the definition formulated in 1916:

> Sculpture as an art is that branch of the free fine arts which chisels or carves out of stone or other solid material or models in clay or other plastic substance for subsequent reproduction by carving or casting, *imitations of natural objects* [emphasis added], chiefly the human form, and represents such objects in their true proportions of length, breadth, and thickness, or of length and breadth only. (*United States v. Olivotti & Co.*, 1916)

During the course of the trial, expert witnesses testified for both sides. Among those who spoke against Brancusi's claim were Robert Ingersoll Aitken and Thomas Hudson Jones. Aitken would later carve the neoclassical West pediment sculpture for the Supreme Court building in Washington, DC. Jones would carve the neoclassical Tomb of the Unknown Soldier in Arlington National Cemetery. Among those who testified on behalf of Brancusi were sculptor Jacob Epstein and Edward Steichen. Epstein was a noted abstract sculptor, and Steichen a photographer and collector of Brancusi's work. In the end, Judge Byron S. Waite found in favor of Brancusi, noting that the acceptable definition of art had broadened to include non-representational art (Hartshorne, 1986). Brancusi's work was ideally suited for testing the concept (it was sufficiently abstract and refined to appear unobtrusively in *Star Wars Episode II: Attack of the Clones* within the apartment of Senator Amidala on the planet of Coruscant).

In this lesson, without necessarily revealing the denouement, the teacher will present the facts of the case of Brancusi and then engage the class in a discussion of "What is art?" In the course of the discussion, the teacher will challenge definitions to broaden the understanding of the pluralistic nature of the concept and how it is bound by communities and subcommunities. For images, teachers may include the works by the experts involved in the case, as well as works by Marcel Duchamp and Auguste Rodin. One could also include *Unique Forms of Continuity in Space* (1913) by Futurist artist Umberto Boccioni, or Wassily Kandinsky's *Improvisation 28 (Second Version)* (1912).

One helpful reading to prepare for teaching this lesson is the chapter "But Is It Art?" in Stephen Law's (2003) wonderful book *The Philosophy Gym*. Among the definitions he succinctly presents are:

- Art as imitation
- Art as expression
- Art expresses beauty
- Art entertains us
- Art has no purpose
- Art must be worked on
- Art has a message about humanity
- Art must be accepted by members of the art world: artists, gallery owners, critics, museum curators (pp. 92–102)

This book also presents Wittgenstein's idea of family resemblance when attempting to define concepts like art.

The class conversation will again be part debate, part discussion, and part maieutic questioning in the form of posing hypotheticals (see Figure 4, p. 48).

LEARNING OBJECTIVES

- Students will consider the following knowledge questions:
  - What is art?
  - Who decides what is art?
  - What is the relationship between the artist, the audience, and the artwork?

- Students will discuss and reflect upon the connections between the arts, the individual, and knowledge communities.

STARTER

Ask students, working in pairs, to define *art*. Remind them that there are three ways to define: with synonyms, with examples, and by an analytical definition. Common responses may include: Art expresses the emotion of the artist; art is whatever the artist says is art; there is no answer. Students will share these answers during the course of the discussion.

MAIN LESSON

Present the law case of *Brancusi v. United States* (1928). Then, conduct a discussion about the case, using the following questions and hypotheticals.

Content and Exploratory Questions:
- ▸ What are the key facts of the case?
- ▸ Was the customs official right in applying the tariff?
- ▸ What was the key concept in the definition of art written into the law?
- ▸ Do you agree with this definition? How would you improve it?
- ▸ If the customs official had applied your definition, what would have happened?
- ▸ What made the judge change his mind about the definition of art?
- ▸ What qualifications make someone an expert on art?
- ▸ If the experts disagree, why should a judge prefer one side to the other? How does he or she decide who is right?
- ▸ What is your own definition of art? How would you decide the case on the basis of your definition?

Hypotheticals/Exploratory Questions:
- ▸ Title and Meaning
  - ▹ What does the title of the sculpture lead you to imagine?
  - ▹ Suppose the title focused on a specific bird (e.g., *Sparrow in Space*). How would this change the meaning?
  - ▹ Suppose the word *Flight* were used instead of *Space*. How would this change the meaning?
  - ▹ From what category of language does *Space* come? Is the artist relating the object to physics through the title?
  - ▹ Suppose one renames the sculpture with a title taken from music, such as *Prelude: Sunrise*. Would this clash with the form of the sculpture? Is it wrong to rename the work?

▷ Suppose the work had no title. Would it have meaning?

▷ Does *Bird in Space* have a specific meaning? What would it be?

▷ Should *Bird in Space* have a message? Does art need a message?

▷ Is abstract art analogous to instrumental music? Does abstract art have a meaning that cannot be pinned down in words but instead can only be experienced?

▶ Work

▷ Is the work beautiful? What formal properties contribute to its beauty?

▷ Suppose the work were considered ugly. Would be it still be considered art?

▷ Suppose Brancusi claimed that the work expressed emotion. Would this be enough to define it as art? What would the emotion be?

▷ Suppose the work were larger. How would that change the experience of the art?

▷ Suppose there were 1,000 identical reproductions of this work. Would the work's meaning and value change? Does the rarity of the work influence its value?

▷ Suppose the 1,000 identical reproductions were very small and could fit in your pocket. Would the meaning and value of the work change?

▷ Suppose each of the 1,000 identical reproductions had a little ring attached and functioned as a key ring. Would the meaning and value of the work change?

▷ Does the work enjoy a kind of integrity or identity related to the many judgments that Brancusi made in fashioning it?

▶ Artist

▷ What gave Brancusi credibility as an artist?

▷ If Brancusi had not studied art in Paris and worked with Rodin, would he then have less credibility?

▷ Suppose Brancusi had no art education or training. Would his art be less credible?

▷ Is it important to see Brancusi's sculpture in a continuum of art? Does it need to fit somehow to qualify as art?

▷ Does the artist take on his identity as an artist from membership within a group of like-minded artists? Does he take on his identity from those people who share the same convictions about art?

▶ Place

▷ Was it important that Brancusi was shipping the work to a collector or an exhibition in a gallery?

▷ Does the fact that the work would be exhibited contribute to its identity as art?

▷ Does the gallery itself, as the place where the object is seen, confer the identity of art?

▷ If someone pays a great deal of money for the sculpture, does the payment confer on the object legitimacy as art?

▷ Suppose Brancusi simply wished to exhibit the work in a metro stop or on the sidewalk. Would it have the same value?

▷ Suppose Marcel Duchamp were shipping *Fountain* (1917) and speaking with a customs office. How would he justify the work as art?

▷ How is *Bird in Flight* the same and different from *Fountain*?

PLENARY

Have students write a reflection considering one or more of the following questions:

▸ What is art?

▸ Who decides what art is?

▸ Must the government respect the freedom of expression of the artist even when there is controversy regarding the status of a work as art? Is there a prioritizing of competing values?

ABOUT THE AUTHOR

Erick Wilberding, Ph.D., is head of the Philosophy Department at Marymount International School in Rome. He received his doctorate in the History of Art from the Institute of Fine Arts of New York University.

For Product Safety Concerns and Information please contact our EU
representative GPSR@taylorandfrancis.com Taylor & Francis Verlag GmbH,
Kaufingerstraße 24, 80331 München, Germany

Printed and bound by CPI Group (UK) Ltd, Croydon, CR0 4YY

08/06/2025

01897013-0002